WORDIE
PUZZLES

WORDIE

PUZZLES

Fantastic Puzzles for the Word Lover

This edition published in 2022 by Arcturus Publishing Limited
26/27 Bickels Yard, 151–153 Bermondsey Street,
London SE1 3HA

AD010966NT

Printed in the UK

1   Word Ladder

Change one letter at a time (but not the position of any letter) to make a new word – and move from the word at the top of the ladder to the word at the bottom using the exact number of rungs provided.

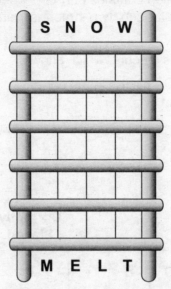

S N O W

M E L T

2   Word Wheel

Using the letters in the wheel, you have ten minutes to find as many words as possible of three or more letters, none of which may be plurals, foreign words or proper nouns.

Each word must contain the central letter and no letters can be used more than once per word unless they appear in different sections of the wheel.

There is at least one nine-letter word to be found.

Nine-letter word(s):

3 The Bottom Line

Can you fill each square in the bottom line with the correct letter, to make a four-letter word?

Every square in the solution contains only one letter from each of the numbered lines above, although two or more squares in the solution may contain the same letter.

At the end of every line is a score, which shows:

a the number of letters placed in the correct finishing position on the bottom line; and

b the number of letters that appear on the bottom line, but in a different position.

					Correctly Placed	Incorrectly Placed
1	M	O	S	T	0	0
2	L	A	U	O	0	1
3	O	A	S	E	1	0
4	U	O	A	N	0	2
5	E	L	D	T	0	2
					4	0

Keyword

On the face of it, this puzzle is perfectly straightforward. Simply fill in the letters missing from words 1-10 and enter them into the numbered boxes, to reveal the hidden keyword.

However, it's possible to have more than one choice of letter for many of the words, so don't fill in the boxes in the keyword until you are quite sure!

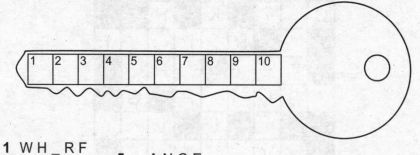

1 WH _ RF
2 AF _ IX
3 ASSE _
4 B _ AST

5 _ ANGE
6 P _ ALM
7 SLOT _

8 RO _ ST
9 S _ ORE

10 BROO _

On the Tiles

Fit the eight tiles into the pattern, to form four words reading across and five words reading down. No tile may be rotated.

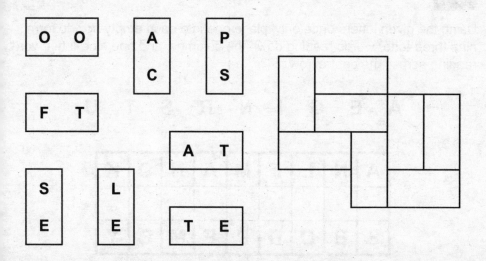

Missing Vowels

All the vowels in this crossword have been removed. Can you replace them, using exactly the quantity shown below?

A A A A A A A

E E E E E E E E E

I I I I

O O O O O

Nine Threes

Using the given letters once only, place one into each empty box, to form nine three-letter words reading down the columns, and one nine-letter word reading across the central row.

A E G I N R S T U

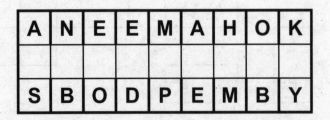

Dice Section

Printed onto every one of the six numbered dice are six letters (one per face), that can be rearranged to form the answer to each clue; however, some sides are invisible to you. Use the clues and write every answer into the grid.

When correctly filled, the letters in the shaded squares, reading in the order 1 to 6, will spell out the name of a creature.

1 Measure of liquid

2 Headgear for a horse

3 Major river of Brazil

4 Distilled wine

5 Croaky

6 Up-to-date

Red Herring

Five of the words below must be entered in the grid, reading across, so as to create five more words reading down. Two letters are already in place. Can you spot the red herring?

AGREE   MESSY

IMAGE   PAPAW

LAIRD   SLAVE

10   Three, Four, Ten

Place each group of three letters into the shaded squares, keeping their letters in order, so that three four-letter words are formed in each row.

Some groups of letters will fit into more than one place, but only the correct combination will lead to four ten-letter words reading down the columns topped by a star.

☆			☆			☆			☆		
D	U	M				E	X	F			
A	L	G				N	D	I			
B	O	U				E	W	I			
O	A	T				T	Y	G			
P	U	F				U	D	A			
T	A	X				V	A	A			
C	Y	A				A	W	B			
V	I	E				O	P	A			
W	A	K				N	X	F			
H	E	I				Y	X	Z			

- ABE
- ARN
- BUT
- CON
- DFL
- EAL
- EMI
- FSC
- HCI
- IDI
- ILM
- LEA
- LUM
- NCL
- NTO
- PAP
- PSE
- RON
- TAN
- URU

The Bottom Line

Can you fill each square in the bottom line with the correct letter, to make a five-letter word?

Every square in the solution contains only one letter from each of the numbered lines above, although two or more squares in the solution may contain the same letter.

At the end of every line is a score, which shows:

a   the number of letters placed in the correct finishing position on the bottom line; and

b   the number of letters that appear on the bottom line, but in a different position.

						Correctly Placed	Incorrectly Placed
1	B	Y	G	I	E	2	0
2	A	S	B	A	A	0	3
3	A	S	A	B	E	0	3
4	L	S	A	D	L	1	2
5	T	T	S	D	D	1	0
						5	0

12 Egg Timer

Can you complete this puzzle in the time it takes to boil an egg?

The answers to the clues are anagrams of the words immediately above and below, plus or minus one letter.

1 Defended, protected

2 Debated hotly

3 Persuaded

4 Ill-mannered

5 Made well again

6 Cut down

7 Firmly fastened

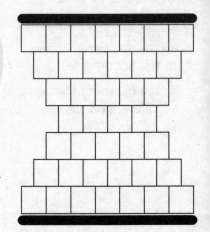

13 Holesome Fun

In this puzzle, you must find a five-letter word by deciding which common letter has been removed from the trios of words. Place that letter into the hole at the end of each row and the answer will be revealed reading downward.

_ O O M	S _ O T	P E _ T	◯
W _ R K	P _ L L	W _ R D	◯
_ O R M	S I _ T	_ O O L	◯
_ R I M	P A S _	_ I L L	◯
W H E _	K E _ S	_ E L L	◯

Couplets

The picture is of a central circle surrounded by shapes, linked to form six sets of three shapes apiece. Can you complete the puzzle by placing each of the two-letter groups below, one per shape, so that every set of three (the central circle, plus the two matching shapes diagonally opposite one another) forms a six-letter word?

Whichever pair of letters you place in the central circle will appear in the middle of every word.

RY

LA

EC

TE

XY

PA

ZE

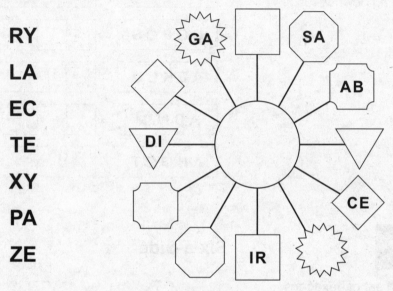

Magic Square

Three letters are already in place in this grid. Use the given letters to fill the empty squares, so that the words reading across are exactly the same as those reading down.

D   E   E   E   E

E   E   G   I   I   L

L   O   P   P   R

R   S   S   T   U   U

16

Drop Out

The letters to the left belong in the squares immediately to the right, but not necessarily in the given order. When entered correctly, they reveal the names of five fruits, reading downwards.

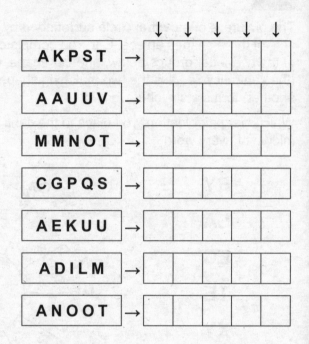

17

Six-a-Side

Each set of hexagons contains a six-letter word, reading around the central number in a clockwise direction.

Each word begins with the letter in the shaded square, and you need to place the missing letter into the empty hexagon.

The inserted letters can then be rearranged to form another six-letter word.

Answer:

_____

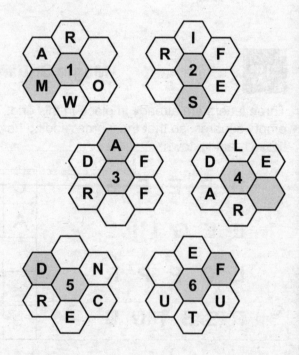

A Novel Approach

Answer the clues by using the groups of letters in the lower box, crossing them out as you go, and placing one letter per square into the grid.

When finished, the remaining letters can be rearranged to make the title of a novel by the author revealed reading down the shaded column.

1 Greet warmly

2 Egg white

3 Large marine crustacean

4 Disciple of Saint Paul

5 Cut off the sun's light

6 Recently enlisted soldier

7 Day of rest and worship

8 Admit one's guilt

9 Mountain in northern Greece

10 Violent whirlwind

11 Reflect a flickering light

Novel: _____

TO	ME	TER	ESS	IP	UM	MOT	US
TI	IDE	IT	KLE	WE	THE	ATH	TW
RNA	OLY	LCO	ECL	AMM	CRU	EN	NF
SA	ALB	BR	DO	BS	IN	CO	OOR
ERM	BB	HY	MP	RE	LO	OFL	SE

The Bottom Line

Can you fill each square in the bottom line with the correct letter, to make a four-letter word?

Every square in the solution contains only one letter from each of the numbered lines above, although two or more squares in the solution may contain the same letter.

At the end of every line is a score, which shows:

a the number of letters placed in the correct finishing position on the bottom line; and

b the number of letters that appear on the bottom line, but in a different position.

					Correctly Placed	Incorrectly Placed
1	S	A	N	G	0	1
2	N	S	E	A	0	1
3	S	O	R	B	2	0
4	D	E	B	N	1	0
5	E	D	T	O	0	2
					4	0

Words Apart

Use the groups of letters on the right to complete the nine-letter words in each row, writing one letter into each square in the order in which they appear. All groups must be used. When the grid is correctly filled, reading down the shaded columns will spell out a two-word phrase.

						I	E	R	WAT	THI
						R	O	R	STR	ORI
						H	E	D	QUE	PHE
						C	A	L	PRO	GAD
						N	E	R	UNE	ANG
						A	T	E	FOR	CON
						T	I	C	BRI	ERS
						E	S	T	GIN	EIG

Downwords

The answers to the clues are all nine-letter words, the letters of which are contained in the grid below, at the rate of one per row in the correct order. Every square is used once only.

1 Tenth sign of the zodiac
2 Maze
3 Identical copy
4 Capital of Iceland
5 Place of refuge or safety
6 Largest island in the northern hemisphere
7 Former name of Cambodia
8 Group of instrumentalists
9 Marine creature with stinging tentacles

C	D	G	J	K	O	L	R	S
A	A	A	A	E	E	R	R	U
B	C	E	L	M	N	P	P	Y
C	E	H	K	L	L	P	R	Y
E	I	I	J	N	R	T	U	Y
A	C	C	C	F	I	L	S	U
A	A	A	H	I	N	O	T	V
E	I	N	R	R	R	S	T	T
A	A	D	E	H	H	K	N	Y

Alphabet Soup

Fill each of the empty squares of this grid with a different letter of the alphabet. Cross off the letters below as you use them.

Out of Place

Place all of the missing letters into the grid, one letter in each empty square to create words that read across and down. Every letter must be placed somewhere within the row or column against which it appears.

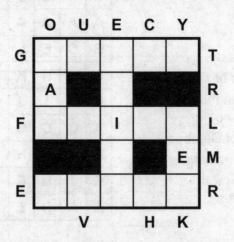

Step by Step

When the seven listed words are correctly placed in the horizontal rows, one letter per square, two more words will be revealed reading down the highlighted steps top left to bottom right, and top right to bottom left. Some letters are already in place.

ALLERGY   MUSICAL

CAPTURE   SPECIAL

CLIMATE   UGLIEST

EMBRACE

Three Down

Fit six of the nine listed words into the horizontal rows in the grid, so that the remaining three words read down the shaded columns.

BABOON   ENZYME   PORTER

CHARGE   KNOTTY   QUARTZ

ELAPSE   LAUNCH   SCREAM

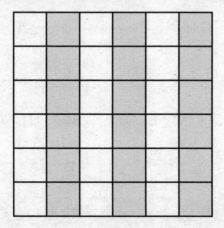

Pyragram

The answer on each level of the pyramid is a single word that is an anagram of the letters in the clue to the left. Place one letter per square in order to reveal the word reading down the shaded column.

1 Don
2 Elbow
3 Rome cap
4 Orchestra
5 Graceful tin
6 Mushy merchant

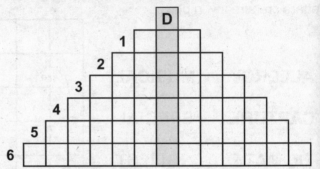

Consonant Hunt

Twelve musical instruments have had their consonants removed; can you put them all back in their proper places?

Use each of the given letters once only.

B B C C C C C C D G H H K L L L L L

M M M N N N N N N N N N N P P P R

R R R S S S T T T T V X

1 _ A _ _ O _ I _ A

2 _ A _ _ O U _ I _ E

3 _ I A _ O

4 _ A _ O _ _ O _ E

5 _ O _ _ E _ _ I _ A

6 U _ U _ E _ E

7 _ I O _ I _

8 _ _ A _ I _ E _

9 _ A _ _ O O _

10 _ U I _ A _

11 _ A _ _ O _ I _

12 _ I _ _ O _ O

Alphafill

Place 25 different letters of the alphabet, one per circle, in order to spell out the listed words. Words are formed by moving between adjacent circles along the connecting lines, either horizontally, vertically, or diagonally in any direction.

Begin by crossing out the letters already in place, together with the one letter that doesn't appear in any of the words.

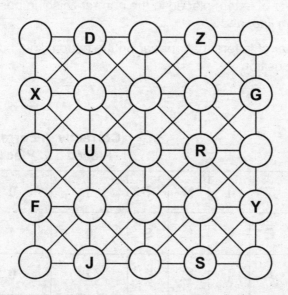

A B C D E F G H I J K L M

N O P Q R S T U V W X Y Z

AVOID	FLUX	QUIVER
BOULES	GRAVEST	SCYTHE
BOX	HELM	WIDOW
DIVERT	JESTER	WIVES
FLESH	PANG	ZANY

The Bottom Line

Can you fill each square in the bottom line with the correct letter, to make a four-letter word?

Every square in the solution contains only one letter from each of the numbered lines above, although two or more squares in the solution may contain the same letter.

At the end of every line is a score, which shows:

a   the number of letters placed in the correct finishing position on the bottom line; and

b   the number of letters that appear on the bottom line, but in a different position.

					Correctly Placed	Incorrectly Placed
1	T	I	N	T	1	0
2	E	E	L	S	0	1
3	A	I	L	K	1	0
4	G	T	S	N	1	1
5	E	U	I	K	2	0
					4	0

Word Ladder

Change one letter at a time (but not the position of any letter) to make a new word – and move from the word at the top of the ladder to the word at the bottom using the exact number of rungs provided.

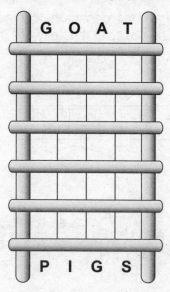

30

Word Wheel

Using the letters in the wheel, you have ten minutes to find as many words as possible of three or more letters, none of which may be plurals, foreign words or proper nouns.

Each word must contain the central letter and no letters can be used more than once per word unless they appear in different sections of the wheel.

There is at least one nine-letter word to be found.

Nine-letter word(s):

_____

Keyword

On the face of it, this puzzle is perfectly straightforward. Simply fill in the letters missing from words 1-10 and enter them into the numbered boxes, to reveal the hidden keyword.

However, it's possible to have more than one choice of letter for many of the words, so don't fill in the boxes in the keyword until you are quite sure!

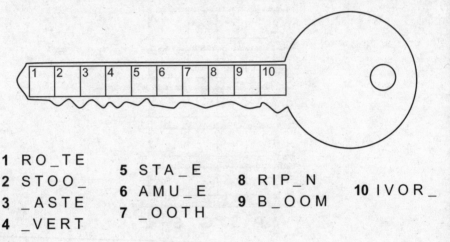

| 1 | 2 | 3 | 4 | 5 | 6 | 7 | 8 | 9 | 10 |

1 RO_TE
2 STOO_
3 _ASTE
4 _VERT

5 STA_E
6 AMU_E
7 _OOTH

8 RIP_N
9 B_OOM

10 IVOR_

On the Tiles

Fit the eight tiles into the pattern, to form four words reading across and five words reading down. No tile may be rotated.

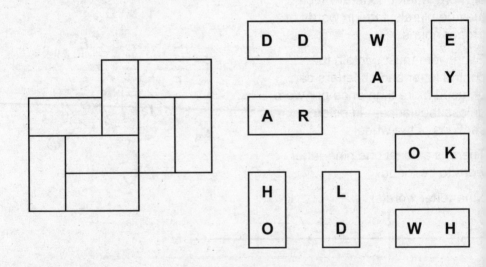

Missing Vowels

All the vowels in this crossword have been removed. Can you replace them, using exactly the quantity shown below?

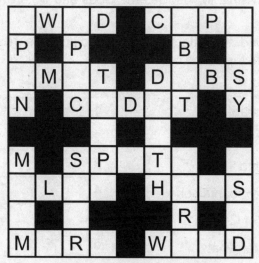

A A A A A A A
E E E E E E E E
I I
O O O O O
U U U U

Nine Threes

Using the given letters once only, place one into each empty box, to form nine three-letter words reading down the columns, and one nine-letter word reading across the central row.

A C D I K R S T Y

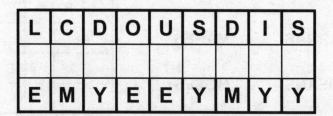

Dice Section

Printed onto every one of the six numbered dice are six letters (one per face), that can be rearranged to form the answer to each clue; however, some sides are invisible to you. Use the clues and write every answer into the grid.

When correctly filled, the letters in the shaded squares, reading in the order 1 to 6, will spell out the name of a fruit.

1 Lucky charm

2 Resist separation

3 Come into view

4 Ice cream container

5 Capital of Croatia

6 No matter what

1   2   3   4   5   6

Red Herring

Five of the words below must be entered in the grid, reading across, so as to create five more words reading down. Two letters are already in place. Can you spot the red herring?

ANISE   MAGMA

ARRAS   MANES

DEANS   MOSES

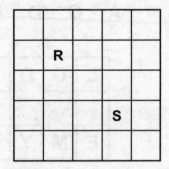

Three, Four, Ten

Place each group of three letters into the shaded squares, keeping their letters in order, so that three four-letter words are formed in each row.

Some groups of letters will fit into more than one place, but only the correct combination will lead to four ten-letter words reading down the columns topped by a star.

☆						☆		☆		☆
W	A	R				S	O	A		
E	C	H				S	H	H		
W	R	E				O	K	I		
D	I	V				O	E	S		
V	E	E				L	T	W		
L	A	I				E	W	J		
W	I	S				A	R	O		
Y	E	T				R	K	E		
P	I	G				N	E	S		
J	U	S				U	A	T		

- AIR
- AOB
- BET
- CAN
- CBR
- HAJ
- IPA
- KIM
- MAL
- NAM
- NCA
- OBU
- PAL
- RAP
- RBE
- SAC
- TSK
- TUI
- UDO
- YPE

The Bottom Line

Can you fill each square in the bottom line with the correct letter, to make a four-letter word?

Every square in the solution contains only one letter from each of the numbered lines above, although two or more squares in the solution may contain the same letter.

At the end of every line is a score, which shows:

a the number of letters placed in the correct finishing position on the bottom line; and

b the number of letters that appear on the bottom line, but in a different position.

					Correctly Placed	Incorrectly Placed
1	S	I	L	O	0	2
2	B	O	O	O	1	0
3	C	D	H	L	1	1
4	D	E	B	L	1	0
5	I	E	W	L	2	0
					4	0

Egg Timer

Can you complete this puzzle in the time it takes to boil an egg?

The answers to the clues are anagrams of the words immediately above and below, plus or minus one letter.

1 Relating to heat
2 Shakespearean play, set in Denmark
3 Material derived from ore
4 Squad
5 Bred
6 Bicycle made for two
7 Wild

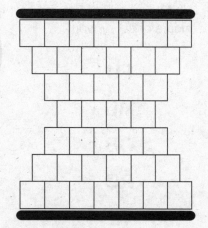

Holesome Fun

In this puzzle, you must find a five-letter word by deciding which common letter has been removed from the trios of words. Place that letter into the hole at the end of each row and the answer will be revealed reading downward.

POS_	_ANG	RIF_	◯
FU_Y	WI_E	MA_K	◯
TH_N	Z_NY	_CHE	◯
_INK	A_AY	YA_N	◯
AB_E	_AMP	FOA_	◯

Couplets

The picture is of a central circle surrounded by shapes, linked to form six sets of three shapes apiece. Can you complete the puzzle by placing each of the two-letter groups below, one per shape, so that every set of three (the central circle, plus the two matching shapes diagonally opposite one another) forms a six-letter word?

Whichever pair of letters you place in the central circle will appear in the middle of every word.

FU

MU

OB

RO

TE

TU

RN

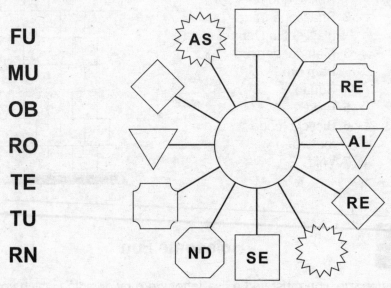

Magic Square

Three letters are already in place in this grid. Use the given letters to fill the empty squares, so that the words reading across are exactly the same as those reading down.

A A C C D

D E E E E E

E I I M M O

R R S S T

44

Drop Out

The letters to the left belong in the squares immediately to the right, but not necessarily in the given order. When entered correctly, they reveal the names of five countries, reading downwards.

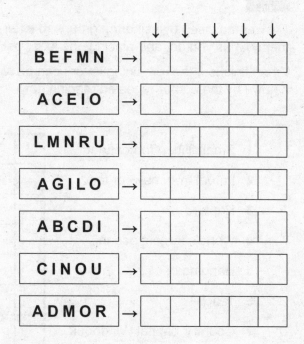

B E F M N	→					
A C E I O	→					
L M N R U	→					
A G I L O	→					
A B C D I	→					
C I N O U	→					
A D M O R	→					

45

Six-a-Side

Each set of hexagons contains a six-letter word, reading around the central number in a clockwise direction.

Each word begins with the letter in the shaded square, and you need to place the missing letter into the empty hexagon.

The inserted letters can then be rearranged to form another six-letter word.

Answer:

_____

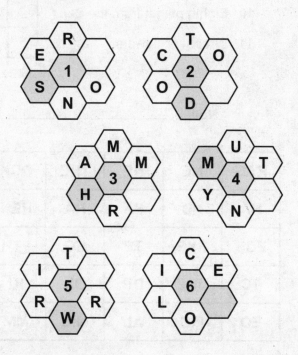

31

A Novel Approach

Answer the clues by using the groups of letters in the lower box, crossing them out as you go, and placing one letter per square into the grid.

When finished, the remaining letters can be rearranged to make the title of a novel by the author revealed reading down the shaded column.

1 Small fish, often canned

2 Larval frog, newt or toad

3 Rapture

4 World's largest ocean

5 Hanging bed

6 Teach

7 Country, capital Windhoek

8 Cooking area

9 Against the law

10 Eighth planet from the Sun

11 Wreath of flowers

Novel: _____

RAG	NE	NE	THE	OCK	IA	ILL	OLE
NA	ND	PA	HA	HEN	RDI	SO	PT
ECS	EYE	TE	EG	FTH	GAR	TA	EDU
TC	UNE	DP	ON	KI	SY	TA	LA
ED	FIC	AL	MIB	MM	CA	SA	CI

The Bottom Line

Can you fill each square in the bottom line with the correct letter, to make a four-letter word?

Every square in the solution contains only one letter from each of the numbered lines above, although two or more squares in the solution may contain the same letter.

At the end of every line is a score, which shows:

a the number of letters placed in the correct finishing position on the bottom line; and

b the number of letters that appear on the bottom line, but in a different position.

					Correctly Placed	Incorrectly Placed
1	S	T	Y	S	0	1
2	M	T	U	R	1	1
3	M	D	T	O	1	2
4	O	T	A	E	1	2
5	Y	T	O	O	0	2
					4	0

Words Apart

Use the groups of letters on the right to complete the nine-letter words in each row, writing one letter into each square in the order in which they appear. All groups must be used. When the grid is correctly filled, reading down the shaded columns will spell out a two-word phrase.

						I	M	E
						U	N	T
						C	E	D
						R	E	D
						I	T	Y
						D	T	H
						T	O	R
						I	A	N

ENT	UNI
DAL	TOM
NSU	RAN
HUN	MAT
PAN	PRO
RAN	HEA
DCO	DRE
XIM	GUA

Downwords

The answers to the clues are all nine-letter words, the letters of which are contained in the grid below, at the rate of one per row in the correct order. Every square is used once only.

1 Emit or release a substance

2 Winged insect

3 Express agreement

4 Creature found in the soil

5 Listen surreptitiously

6 Extremely attractive

7 14th century BC queen of Egypt

8 Ledge in a library

9 Study of celestial bodies and the universe

A	A	B	B	B	D	E	E	N
A	A	C	E	E	I	O	S	U
A	F	O	Q	R	S	T	T	V
C	E	E	K	R	T	T	U	U
E	H	H	I	O	R	S	S	T
A	D	E	H	I	N	R	T	W
E	F	F	I	O	O	R	R	S
C	G	L	L	M	O	R	T	U
E	E	F	I	L	M	P	Y	Y

Alphabet Soup

Fill each of the empty squares of this grid with a different letter of the alphabet. Cross off the letters below as you use them.

A
B
C
D
E
F
G
H
I
J
K
L
M

C		R	D			F		
A		A		C	A		A	A	N
T	A		S		G		R		N
A		S		U	E	A	M			
			U		L		S			O
	C	E	A			O		T	E	R
M			W				E			S
B	A	C			E	D	A	L		
	N		I		W		D	A		B
	E	A	N		E	R				O
			G				L		N	

N
O
P
Q
R
S
T
U
V
W
X
Y
Z

Out of Place

Place all of the missing letters into the grid, one letter in each empty square to create words that read across and down. Every letter must be placed somewhere within the row or column against which it appears.

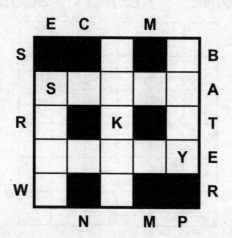

35

Step by Step

When the seven listed words are correctly placed in the horizontal rows, one letter per square, two more words will be revealed reading down the highlighted steps top left to bottom right, and top right to bottom left. Some letters are already in place.

ANARCHY   METHANE

COCKPIT   SEGMENT

DUCKING   THYROID

MILLION

			M			
						Y
M						
		K				

Three Down

Fit six of the nine listed words into the horizontal rows in the grid, so that the remaining three words read down the shaded columns.

AEGEAN   INFANT   PIGEON
DECAMP   JUGGLE   PLENTY
EQUINE   KEENLY   SQUEAL

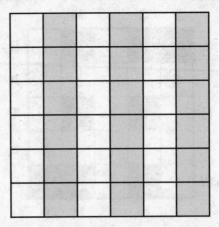

54   Pyragram

The answer on each level of the pyramid is a single word that is an anagram of the letters in the clue to the left. Place one letter per square in order to reveal the word reading down the shaded column.

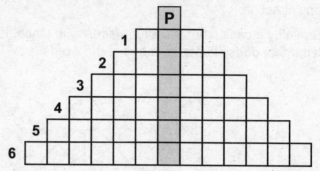

1 Run

2 Aloft

3 On Earth

4 His cattle

5 Current time

6 Internal venom

55   Consonant Hunt

Twelve gemstones have had their consonants removed; can you put them all back in their proper places?

Use each of the given letters once only.

**B B D D D H H L L L M M M M N
N N P P P P Q Q R R R R R R R S
S S T T T T T T Y Y Y Z**

1 _IA_O_ _

2 _A_ _ _I_E

3 E_E_A_ _

4 _E_I_O_

5 A_E_ _ _ _ _

6 _O_A_

7 _U_ _

8 _E_ _ _

9 _OU_ _A_I_E

10 A_UA_A_I_E

11 O_A_

12 _U_ _UOI_E

37

Alphafill

Place 25 different letters of the alphabet, one per circle, in order to spell out the listed words. Words are formed by moving between adjacent circles along the connecting lines, either horizontally, vertically, or diagonally in any direction.

Begin by crossing out the letters already in place, together with the one letter that doesn't appear in any of the words.

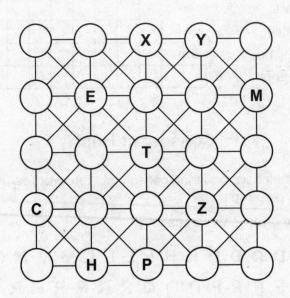

A B C D E F G H I J K L M

N O P Q R S T U V W X Y Z

BRUTAL	MAGAZINE	POND
CONVEX	MARTIN	SKIP
EQUATE	NOTARY	SLATED
HONED	PHOTON	TUXEDO
JOINT	POINTED	WENCH

The Bottom Line

Can you fill each square in the bottom line with the correct letter, to make a four-letter word?

Every square in the solution contains only one letter from each of the numbered lines above, although two or more squares in the solution may contain the same letter.

At the end of every line is a score, which shows:

a the number of letters placed in the correct finishing position on the bottom line; and

b the number of letters that appear on the bottom line, but in a different position.

					Correctly Placed	Incorrectly Placed
1	L	I	C	E	0	3
2	A	V	E	C	0	2
3	C	O	L	I	0	2
4	E	V	W	C	0	2
5	W	O	V	E	0	2
					4	0

58   Word Ladder

Change one letter at a time (but not the position of any letter) to make a new word – and move from the word at the top of the ladder to the word at the bottom using the exact number of rungs provided.

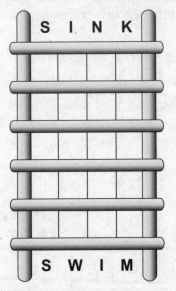

59   Word Wheel

Using the letters in the wheel, you have ten minutes to find as many words as possible of three or more letters, none of which may be plurals, foreign words or proper nouns.

Each word must contain the central letter and no letters can be used more than once per word unless they appear in different sections of the wheel.

There is at least one nine-letter word to be found.

Nine-letter word(s):

Keyword

On the face of it, this puzzle is perfectly straightforward. Simply fill in the letters missing from words 1-10 and enter them into the numbered boxes, to reveal the hidden keyword.

However, it's possible to have more than one choice of letter for many of the words, so don't fill in the boxes in the keyword until you are quite sure!

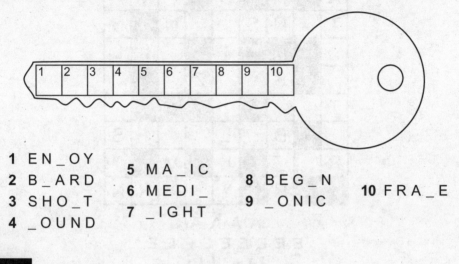

1 EN _ OY
2 B _ ARD
3 SHO _ T
4 _ OUND

5 MA _ IC
6 MEDI _
7 _ IGHT

8 BEG _ N
9 _ ONIC

10 FRA _ E

On the Tiles

Fit the eight tiles into the pattern, to form four words reading across and five words reading down. No tile may be rotated.

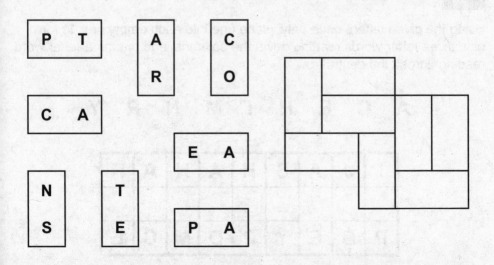

41

Missing Vowels

All the vowels in this crossword have been removed. Can you replace them, using exactly the quantity shown below?

A A A A

E E E E E E E E E

I I I I I I I

O O O O O O

U U U

Nine Threes

Using the given letters once only, place one into each empty box, to form nine three-letter words reading down the columns, and one nine-letter word reading across the central row.

A C E H I M N R Y

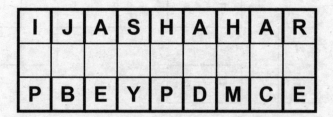

I	J	A	S	H	A	H	A	R
P	B	E	Y	P	D	M	C	E

Dice Section

Printed onto every one of the six numbered dice are six letters (one per face), that can be rearranged to form the answer to each clue; however, some sides are invisible to you. Use the clues and write every answer into the grid.

When correctly filled, the letters in the shaded squares, reading in the order 1 to 6, will spell out the name of a flower.

1 Book of the Bible
2 Alter
3 Item that prevents a ship from moving
4 Small whale, a source of caviar
5 Sign of the zodiac
6 Imperfect

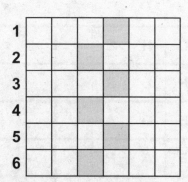

1   2   3   4   5   6

Red Herring

Five of the words below must be entered in the grid, reading across, so as to create five more words reading down. Two letters are already in place. Can you spot the red herring?

ASSET   ESTER

BEAUS   ORLON

CAPRI   RANGE

R

G

Three, Four, Ten

Place each group of three letters into the shaded squares, keeping their letters in order, so that three four-letter words are formed in each row.

Some groups of letters will fit into more than one place, but only the correct combination will lead to four ten-letter words reading down the columns topped by a star.

			☆		☆				☆		☆
C	H	E				E	X	K			
H	E	R				C	K	V			
B	O	A				A	M	A			
F	A	R				E	W	C			
M	A	G				O	G	S			
C	L	O				E	W	E			
C	O	L				K	E	T			
G	R	A				R	F	U			
C	O	W				A	W	V			
W	I	F				E	A	A			

- AJO
- AXI
- BTU
- DBR
- EID
- EIN
- FIB
- GAR
- HUB
- IAG
- ISA
- LGN
- MIR
- MSK
- NOB
- OPA
- REA
- RSC
- SKS
- TOA

The Bottom Line

Can you fill each square in the bottom line with the correct letter, to make a four-letter word?

Every square in the solution contains only one letter from each of the numbered lines above, although two or more squares in the solution may contain the same letter.

At the end of every line is a score, which shows:

a the number of letters placed in the correct finishing position on the bottom line; and

b the number of letters that appear on the bottom line, but in a different position.

					Correctly Placed	Incorrectly Placed
1	O	V	A	L	0	1
2	E	P	G	O	0	1
3	G	S	V	V	0	1
4	S	L	E	A	0	2
5	O	O	P	P	0	1
					4	0

68   Egg Timer

Can you complete this puzzle in the time it takes to boil an egg?

The answers to the clues are anagrams of the words immediately above and below, plus or minus one letter.

1 Carrying

2 Get back

3 Ire

4 Toothed wheel

5 Tally

6 Treat, entertain

7 Comprehensive

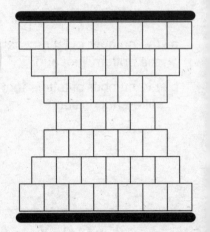

69   Holesome Fun

In this puzzle, you must find a five-letter word by deciding which common letter has been removed from the trios of words. Place that letter into the hole at the end of each row and the answer will be revealed reading downward.

L _ C E	I D E _	_ L L Y	◯
D O _ E	Q U I _	_ I N C	◯
_ L N A	C _ R T	M E N _	◯
L I A _	_ O A D	A _ I D	◯
S L _ W	_ T C H	B O N _	◯

Couplets

The picture is of a central circle surrounded by shapes, linked to form six sets of three shapes apiece. Can you complete the puzzle by placing each of the two-letter groups below, one per shape, so that every set of three (the central circle, plus the two matching shapes diagonally opposite one another) forms a six-letter word?

Whichever pair of letters you place in the central circle will appear in the middle of every word.

AT

CO

DI

NT

RE

RN

VE

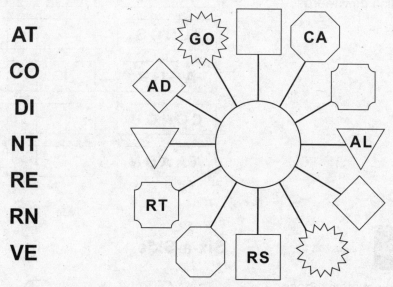

Magic Square

Three letters are already in place in this grid. Use the given letters to fill the empty squares, so that the words reading across are exactly the same as those reading down.

A A D D D

D E E E E

H H O O O

R R S S S

Drop Out

The letters to the left belong in the squares immediately to the right, but not necessarily in the given order. When entered correctly, they reveal the names of five islands, reading downwards.

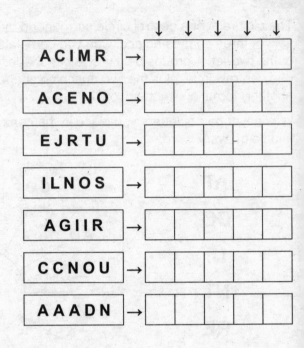

| ↓ | ↓ | ↓ | ↓ | ↓ |

A C I M R →

A C E N O →

E J R T U →

I L N O S →

A G I I R →

C C N O U →

A A A D N →

Six-a-Side

Each set of hexagons contains a six-letter word, reading around the central number in a clockwise direction.

Each word begins with the letter in the shaded square, and you need to place the missing letter into the empty hexagon.

The inserted letters can then be rearranged to form another six-letter word.

Answer:

_____

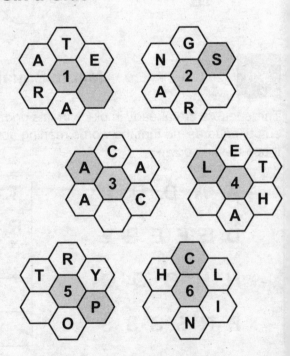

48

A Novel Approach

Answer the clues by using the groups of letters in the lower box, crossing them out as you go, and placing one letter per square into the grid.

When finished, the remaining letters can be rearranged to make the title of a novel by the author revealed reading down the shaded column.

1 Former name of Benin

2 Lack, deficiency

3 Falls on the Canada/US border

4 Country, capital Reykjavik

5 Green gem

6 Wool fat

7 Unit of sound intensity

8 Breathed out

9 At last

10 Shape with eight sides

11 Interlace

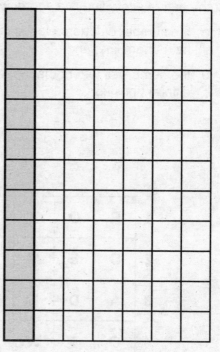

Novel: _____

AG	EN	US	OM	IB	BI	OC	IC
HAL	NS	OL	EL	EM	LLY	ON	TAG
AND	EX	ARA	EL	DAH	SEN	TW	LD
CR	IN	NA	RO	ERA	FI	LAN	NI
INE	EY	AB	DEC	ON	OE	ED	CE

The Bottom Line

Can you fill each square in the bottom line with the correct letter, to make a four-letter word?

Every square in the solution contains only one letter from each of the numbered lines above, although two or more squares in the solution may contain the same letter.

At the end of every line is a score, which shows:

a the number of letters placed in the correct finishing position on the bottom line; and

b the number of letters that appear on the bottom line, but in a different position.

					Correctly Placed	Incorrectly Placed
1	R	O	T	E	0	1
2	D	E	M	O	0	1
3	A	D	E	T	0	1
4	O	T	W	D	0	1
5	M	M	A	D	0	2
					4	0

Words Apart

Use the groups of letters on the right to complete the nine-letter words in each row, writing one letter into each square in the order in which they appear. All groups must be used. When the grid is correctly filled, reading down the shaded columns will spell out a two-word phrase.

						O	S	M
						T	H	S
						I	L	L
						A	T	H
						R	C	E
						O	U	S
						F	L	Y
						I	N	E

ROC	HOM
NFO	GON
ADM	BEH
AND	IDU
MIC	REI
EOP	TRE
DRA	CEL
EMO	DEC

Downwords

The answers to the clues are all nine-letter words, the letters of which are contained in the grid below, at the rate of one per row in the correct order. Every square is used once only.

1 Space communication device
2 Not sure
3 Feeling of longing for something past
4 Ludwig van ___, German composer
5 Detonation
6 Open to more than one interpretation
7 Ship in which the Pilgrim Fathers sailed
8 Crystal of frozen rain
9 Escort hired for protection

A	B	B	E	M	N	S	S	U
A	A	E	M	N	N	O	O	X
B	C	D	E	O	P	S	T	Y
E	E	F	I	L	T	T	W	Y
A	F	G	G	H	L	L	O	R
L	L	L	O	O	S	T	U	U
A	A	A	G	I	I	O	V	W
E	E	I	I	K	O	R	T	U
A	D	E	E	N	N	N	R	S

Alphabet Soup

Fill each of the empty squares of this grid with a different letter of the alphabet. Cross off the letters below as you use them.

A   N E A D   S   A   C   N
B   A   U N L U   K Y   O
C   A L   O   H   P
D   T   E   W E E N   Q
E   I G S   I   R
F   C   C   P S   F   S
G   A   U   L   U T   T
H   B   A   D E R   S   U
I   R   W   R   U N   I P   V
J   A   R E A R   W
K   T H R   X
L   Y
M   Z

Out of Place

Place all of the missing letters into the grid, one letter in each empty square to create words that read across and down. Every letter must be placed somewhere within the row or column against which it appears.

80 Step by Step

When the seven listed boys' names are correctly placed in the horizontal rows, one letter per square, another boy's name will be revealed reading down the highlighted steps top left to bottom right. Some letters are already in place.

ANTHONY   **RICHARD**

CLEMENT   **ROYSTON**

GREGORY   **WILFRED**

MAURICE

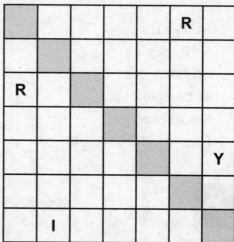

81 Three Down

Fit six of the nine listed words into the horizontal rows in the grid, so that the remaining three words read down the shaded columns.

ADVENT   **FLEECE**   **SPOOKY**
BOOTEE   **MOLTEN**   **THRONG**
CYGNET   **QUEBEC**   **UPHOLD**

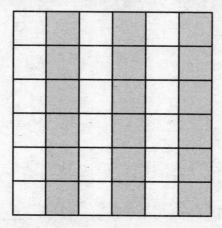

82   Pyragram

The answer on each level of the pyramid is a single word that is an anagram of the letters in the clue to the left. Place one letter per square in order to reveal the word reading down the shaded column.

1 Tip
2 Scale
3 Bed lock
4 Don grew up
5 Old canoeist
6 I command a coot

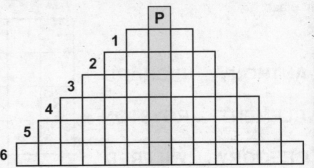

83   Consonant Hunt

Twelve European capital cities have had their consonants removed; can you put them all back in their proper places?

Use each of the given letters once only.

B B B C D D D D G G H H K L L L L

M M M M N N N N N N P P R R R R

R S S S S S S S T T T V V W W Z

1 _ A _ _ I _

2 _ I E _ _ A

3 O _ _ O

4 _ _ A _ I _ _ A _ A

5 _ O _ E _ _ A _ E _

6 _ A _ I _

7 _ I _ _ O _

8 _ _ O _ _ _ O _ _

9 _ A _ _ E _

10 _ A _ _ A _

11 _ O _ _ O _

12 A _ _ _ E _ _ A _

54

Alphafill

Place 25 different letters of the alphabet, one per circle, in order to spell out the listed words. Words are formed by moving between adjacent circles along the connecting lines, either horizontally, vertically, or diagonally in any direction.

Begin by crossing out the letters already in place, together with the one letter that doesn't appear in any of the words.

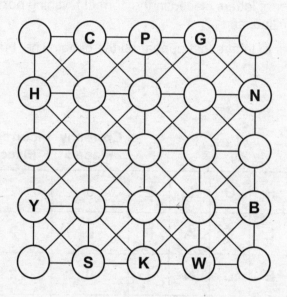

A B C D E F G H I J K L M
N O P Q R S T U V W X Y Z

CHALETS	GLIB	SUET
CLIMB	HALVE	TOMB
CRAZE	LAZY	TUSK
DOTING	MINX	TWO
FUTILE	PLAQUE	VETO

The Bottom Line

Can you fill each square in the bottom line with the correct letter, to make a four-letter word?

Every square in the solution contains only one letter from each of the numbered lines above, although two or more squares in the solution may contain the same letter.

At the end of every line is a score, which shows:

a the number of letters placed in the correct finishing position on the bottom line; and

b the number of letters that appear on the bottom line, but in a different position.

					Correctly Placed	Incorrectly Placed
1	H	O	L	E	0	2
2	L	E	A	P	0	2
3	E	L	N	I	0	2
4	A	N	P	L	0	2
5	N	H	A	O	0	2
					4	0

Word Ladder

Change one letter at a time (but not the position of any letter) to make a new word – and move from the word at the top of the ladder to the word at the bottom using the exact number of rungs provided.

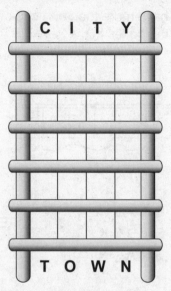

87

Word Wheel

Using the letters in the wheel, you have ten minutes to find as many words as possible of three or more letters, none of which may be plurals, foreign words or proper nouns.

Each word must contain the central letter and no letters can be used more than once per word unless they appear in different sections of the wheel.

There is at least one nine-letter word to be found.

Nine-letter word(s):

_____

88   Keyword

On the face of it, this puzzle is perfectly straightforward. Simply fill in the letters missing from words 1-10 and enter them into the numbered boxes, to reveal the hidden keyword.

However, it's possible to have more than one choice of letter for many of the words, so don't fill in the boxes in the keyword until you are quite sure!

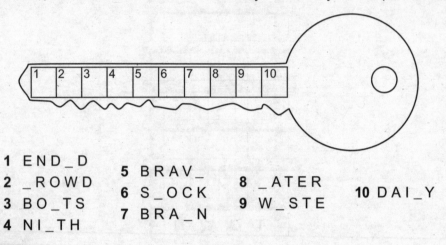

| 1 | 2 | 3 | 4 | 5 | 6 | 7 | 8 | 9 | 10 |

1 END_D
2 _ROWD
3 BO_TS
4 NI_TH

5 BRAV_
6 S_OCK
7 BRA_N

8 _ATER
9 W_STE

10 DAI_Y

89   On the Tiles

Fit the eight tiles into the pattern, to form four words reading across and five words reading down. No tile may be rotated.

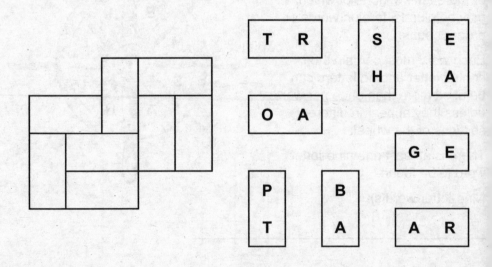

Missing Vowels

All the vowels in this crossword have been removed. Can you replace them, using exactly the quantity shown below?

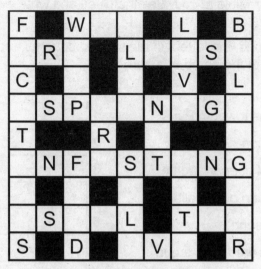

A A A A A A
E E E E E E E E
I I I I I
O O O O O O O
U U U U

Nine Threes

Using the given letters once only, place one into each empty box, to form nine three-letter words reading down the columns, and one nine-letter word reading across the central row.

A I M N O P R S Y

Dice Section

Printed onto every one of the six numbered dice are six letters (one per face), that can be rearranged to form the answer to each clue; however, some sides are invisible to you. Use the clues and write every answer into the grid.

When correctly filled, the letters in the shaded squares, reading in the order 1 to 6, will spell out the name of a herb.

1 Famous tower in Paris

2 Inhalation

3 Alloy of copper and tin

4 European principality

5 Slumbering

6 Missile fired from a gun

1   2   3   4   5   6

Red Herring

Five of the words below must be entered in the grid, reading across, so as to create five more words reading down. Two letters are already in place. Can you spot the red herring?

AGARS   PASTA

EASED   ROLES

KRONA   SANDY

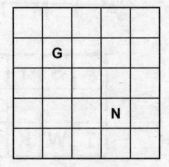

Three, Four, Ten

Place each group of three letters into the shaded squares, keeping their letters in order, so that three four-letter words are formed in each row.

Some groups of letters will fit into more than one place, but only the correct combination will lead to four ten-letter words reading down the columns topped by a star.

☆			☆				☆		☆	
L	I	M			E	T	H			
L	A	V			N	Y	A			
E	V	I			O	G	P			
R	A	N			R	N	J			
D	A	M			U	X	A			
K	I	N			R	B	V			
J	E	E			U	B	G			
H	E	R			F	T	C			
O	V	U			O	K	S			
D	U	K			E	W	K			

- ADE
- AFE
- ARP
- DBA
- EEN
- EKN
- ETO
- IBU
- ILT
- LAG
- LSO
- LUS
- MBO
- OGI
- PFL
- PFR
- RID
- RST
- TAR
- TOM

95   The Bottom Line

Can you fill each square in the bottom line with the correct letter, to make a four-letter word?

Every square in the solution contains only one letter from each of the numbered lines above, although two or more squares in the solution may contain the same letter.

At the end of every line is a score, which shows:

a   the number of letters placed in the correct finishing position on the bottom line; and

b   the number of letters that appear on the bottom line, but in a different position.

					Correctly Placed	Incorrectly Placed
1	A	E	R	Y	0	1
2	L	O	B	S	0	2
3	S	S	E	O	0	2
4	B	E	S	B	0	2
5	E	L	B	A	0	2
					4	0

Egg Timer

Can you complete this puzzle in the time it takes to boil an egg?

The answers to the clues are anagrams of the words immediately above and below, plus or minus one letter.

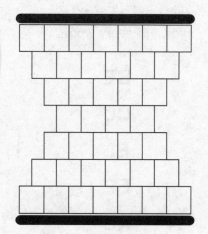

1 Downward movement

2 Sheltered birds,
   for example

3 Thick, solidly packed

4 Despatch

5 Necessities

6 Perceived

7 Eternal

Holesome Fun

In this puzzle, you must find a five-letter word by deciding which common letter has been removed from the trios of words. Place that letter into the hole at the end of each row and the answer will be revealed reading downward.

_ O S T	E P I _	M I _ E	◯
E M I _	_ O S E	P _ O D	◯
E _ E S	B O D _	_ E A R	◯
_ A W S	S _ U N	_ Y R E	◯
B I _ E	_ A N K	E _ C H	◯

Couplets

The picture is of a central circle surrounded by shapes, linked to form six sets of three shapes apiece. Can you complete the puzzle by placing each of the two-letter groups below, one per shape, so that every set of three (the central circle, plus the two matching shapes diagonally opposite one another) forms a six-letter word?

Whichever pair of letters you place in the central circle will appear in the middle of every word.

BE

CU

EL

EP

RO

RU

ST

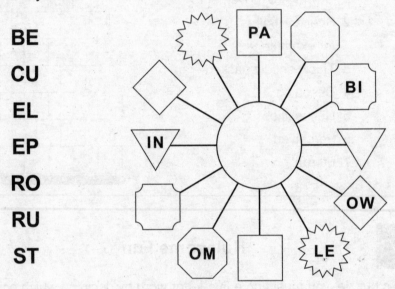

Magic Square

Three letters are already in place in this grid. Use the given letters to fill the empty squares, so that the words reading across are exactly the same as those reading down.

A A A A C

C E E E E H

H J R R R

R S S T T X

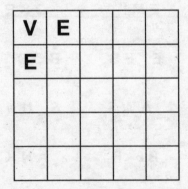

100 Drop Out

The letters to the left belong in the squares immediately to the right, but not necessarily in the given order. When entered correctly, they reveal the names of five animals, reading downwards.

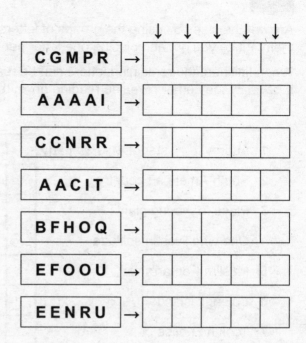

101 Six-a-Side

Each set of hexagons contains a six-letter word, reading around the central number in a clockwise direction.

Each word begins with the letter in the shaded square, and you need to place the missing letter into the empty hexagon.

The inserted letters can then be rearranged to form another six-letter word.

Answer:

_____

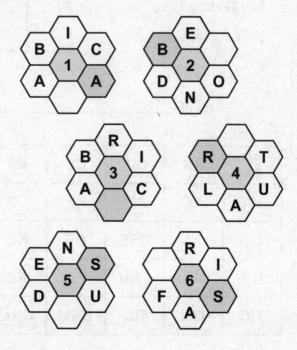

A Novel Approach

Answer the clues by using the groups of letters in the lower box, crossing them out as you go, and placing one letter per square into the grid.

When finished, the remaining letters can be rearranged to make the title of a novel by the author revealed reading down the shaded column.

1 Audrey ____, star of *My Fair Lady*

2 South American country

3 Place for young plants

4 One who lives in solitude

5 Muslim woman's veil

6 Balearic island

7 Took no notice of

8 Cases used to carry belongings

9 Spotted wild cat

10 Stretchy fabric

11 Leisurely, easy-going

Novel: _____

ED	RN	OPI	CL	RE	ECU	LU	LE
RSE	AS	AK	HE	JO	GGA	IGN	APR
CO	IC	USE	GE	NU	TR	LAX	YA
OR	MA	PBU	FC	RE	EL	AD	ED
TIC	OR	RD	SHM	ORN	RY	RCA	OPA

The Bottom Line

Can you fill each square in the bottom line with the correct letter, to make a four-letter word?

Every square in the solution contains only one letter from each of the numbered lines above, although two or more squares in the solution may contain the same letter.

At the end of every line is a score, which shows:

a   the number of letters placed in the correct finishing position on the bottom line; and

b   the number of letters that appear on the bottom line, but in a different position.

					Correctly Placed	Incorrectly Placed
1	M	U	S	T	0	2
2	E	L	O	I	0	2
3	U	E	I	M	0	2
4	I	M	U	S	0	2
5	T	E	M	U	0	2
					4	0

Words Apart

Use the groups of letters on the right to complete the nine-letter words in each row, writing one letter into each square in the order in which they appear. All groups must be used. When the grid is correctly filled, reading down the shaded columns will spell out a two-word phrase.

						U	T	E
						R	U	S
						I	T	H
						C	A	L
						I	T	E
						E	C	E
						O	C	K
						M	A	N

EXT	SAU
RGY	SSI
THE	LIV
RPI	ACH
CLA	HAI
CLE	GOL
DSM	RAD
PAR	EST

Downwords

The answers to the clues are all nine-letter words, the letters of which are contained in the grid below, at the rate of one per row in the correct order. Every square is used once only.

1 Rate of recurrence
2 Charge someone with too many tasks
3 Celebrated in fable
4 Set free
5 At a convenient or suitable time
6 Store for goods and merchandise
7 Lack of knowledge or education
8 Variety of peach
9 Explosive compound

F	G	I	L	L	N	O	O	W
A	E	E	G	I	P	R	U	V
B	C	E	E	G	N	N	P	R
E	E	E	O	O	P	Q	R	T
A	H	N	O	R	R	R	U	W
A	A	D	E	H	O	R	T	W
A	D	E	I	N	N	T	U	U
C	C	E	E	L	N	N	R	S
D	E	E	E	E	M	R	Y	Y

Alphabet Soup

Fill each of the empty squares of this grid with a different letter of the alphabet. Cross off the letters below as you use them.

A
B
C
D
E
F
G
H
I
J
K
L
M

N
O
P
Q
R
S
T
U
V
W
X
Y
Z

Out of Place

Place all of the missing letters into the grid, one letter in each empty square to create words that read across and down. Every letter must be placed somewhere within the row or column against which it appears.

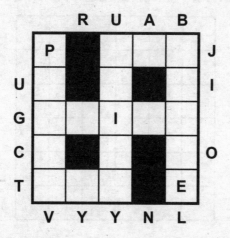

Step by Step

When the seven listed words are correctly placed in the horizontal rows, one letter per square, two more words will be revealed reading down the highlighted steps top left to bottom right, and top right to bottom left. Some letters are already in place.

ARABIAN   NOWHERE

BASSOON   PILGRIM

COSTUME   STIMULI

ETERNAL

Three Down

Fit six of the nine listed words into the horizontal rows in the grid, so that the remaining three words read down the shaded columns.

ARREST   FRIDAY   ISOGON
CRENEL   GEMINI   STRONG
FLYING   INDIGO   TARIFF

Pyragram

The answer on each level of the pyramid is a single word that is an anagram of the letters in the clue to the left. Place one letter per square in order to reveal the word reading down the shaded column.

1 Ton
2 Demit
3 Odd tape
4 Meat menus
5 Fabric in eye
6 Inverted teams

P

1
2
3
4
5
6

Consonant Hunt

Twelve books of the Bible have had their consonants removed; can you put them all back in their proper places?

Use each of the given letters once only.

B B B D D G H H H J J K K L L L M M

M M N N N N P R R R S S S S S S

T T W W X Z

1 E_O_U_

2 _ _A_ _ _

3 _A_ _

4 _U_ _E_ _

5 _U_E

6 _O_A_

7 _O_

8 _E_E_I_

9 E_ _A

10 _E_ _E_ _

11 _A_ _ _E_

12 _A_IE_

Alphafill

Place 25 different letters of the alphabet, one per circle, in order to spell out the listed words. Words are formed by moving between adjacent circles along the connecting lines, either horizontally, vertically, or diagonally in any direction.

Begin by crossing out the letters already in place, together with the one letter that doesn't appear in any of the words.

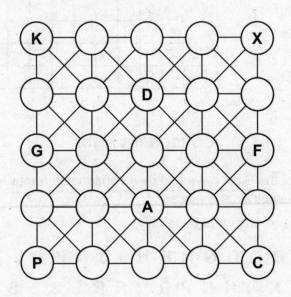

A B C D E F G H I J K L M

N O P Q R S T U V W X Y Z

AVERTED	INDEX	PUMA
COLUMN	JEROBOAM	QUARTER
FRAMING	KING	ROYAL
FRESH	MAUVE	VERB
GUAM	MINK	WAVER

The Bottom Line

Can you fill each square in the bottom line with the correct letter, to make a four-letter word?

Every square in the solution contains only one letter from each of the numbered lines above, although two or more squares in the solution may contain the same letter.

At the end of every line is a score, which shows:

a the number of letters placed in the correct finishing position on the bottom line; and

b the number of letters that appear on the bottom line, but in a different position.

					Correctly Placed	Incorrectly Placed
1	O	M	I	T	0	2
2	U	E	S	R	1	1
3	E	T	U	I	1	1
4	M	E	S	O	0	1
5	I	R	U	M	1	1
					4	0

Word Ladder

Change one letter at a time (but not the position of any letter) to make a new word – and move from the word at the top of the ladder to the word at the bottom using the exact number of rungs provided.

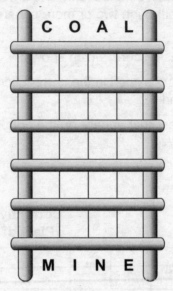

C O A L

M I N E

Word Wheel

Using the letters in the wheel, you have ten minutes to find as many words as possible of three or more letters, none of which may be plurals, foreign words or proper nouns.

Each word must contain the central letter and no letters can be used more than once per word unless they appear in different sections of the wheel.

There is at least one nine-letter word to be found.

Nine-letter word(s):

_____

Keyword

On the face of it, this puzzle is perfectly straightforward. Simply fill in the letters missing from words 1-10 and enter them into the numbered boxes, to reveal the hidden keyword.

However, it's possible to have more than one choice of letter for many of the words, so don't fill in the boxes in the keyword until you are quite sure!

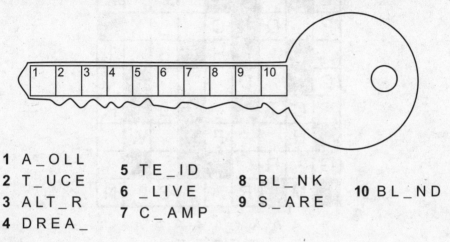

1 A _ OLL

2 T _ UCE

3 ALT _ R

4 DREA _

5 TE _ ID

6 _ LIVE

7 C _ AMP

8 BL _ NK

9 S _ ARE

10 BL _ ND

On the Tiles

Fit the eight tiles into the pattern, to form four words reading across and five words reading down. No tile may be rotated.

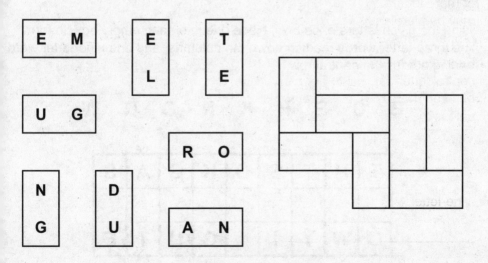

Missing Vowels

All the vowels in this crossword have been removed. Can you replace them, using exactly the quantity shown below?

A A A A A A A A A
E E E E
I I I I
O O O O O O O
U U U U

Nine Threes

Using the given letters once only, place one into each empty box, to form nine three-letter words reading down the columns, and one nine-letter word reading across the central row.

B C E H K N O R W

T	H	T	S	O	K	G	A	S
O	W	Y	I	I	G	U	T	E

Dice Section

Printed onto every one of the six numbered dice are six letters (one per face), that can be rearranged to form the answer to each clue; however, some sides are invisible to you. Use the clues and write every answer into the grid.

When correctly filled, the letters in the shaded squares, reading in the order 1 to 6, will spell out the name of a breed of dog.

1 Floor covering   **1**

2 Foaming   **2**

3 Nearly   **3**

4 Monetary plan   **4**

5 Arthurian magician   **5**

6 Hard-cased arthropod   **6**

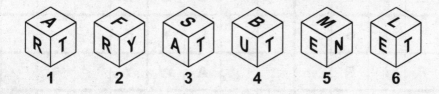

121

Red Herring

Five of the words below must be entered in the grid, reading across, so as to create five more words reading down. Two letters are already in place. Can you spot the red herring?

ADORN   **MATED**

CRESS   **PRESS**

LAMIA   **STRUT**

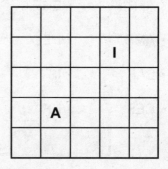

Three, Four, Ten

Place each group of three letters into the shaded squares, keeping their letters in order, so that three four-letter words are formed in each row.

Some groups of letters will fit into more than one place, but only the correct combination will lead to four ten-letter words reading down the columns topped by a star.

			☆						☆		☆
G	L	I				A	R	J			
C	O	I				Z	Z	A			
I	O	T				O	G	S			
E	P	I				P	Y	T			
D	O	C				Z	Z	B			
K	I	S				L	Y	K			
F	I	R				A	W	Y			
K	I	W				Y	E	A			
J	I	L				U	D	W			
H	U	S				G	Y	B			

- AFR
- AMB
- BAF
- CES
- ERE
- HED
- IST
- KFI
- LJA
- MID
- MTH
- NEE
- OGA
- OTH
- RED
- RUE
- SIA
- SUG
- TFE
- TIR

The Bottom Line

Can you fill each square in the bottom line with the correct letter, to make a four-letter word?

Every square in the solution contains only one letter from each of the numbered lines above, although two or more squares in the solution may contain the same letter.

At the end of every line is a score, which shows:

a the number of letters placed in the correct finishing position on the bottom line; and

b the number of letters that appear on the bottom line, but in a different position.

					Correctly Placed	Incorrectly Placed
1	N	I	K	E	0	2
2	O	E	M	I	0	2
3	I	K	A	M	0	2
4	E	S	M	N	0	2
5	S	N	E	O	0	2
					4	0

124   Egg Timer

Can you complete this puzzle in the time it takes to boil an egg?

The answers to the clues are anagrams of the words immediately above and below, plus or minus one letter.

1 Branch of mathematics
2 Cultivatable
3 Harsh trumpeting sound
4 Genuine
5 Transparent
6 Baby's bed
7 Crept on hands and knees

125   Holesome Fun

In this puzzle, you must find a five-letter word by deciding which common letter has been removed from the trios of words. Place that letter into the hole at the end of each row and the answer will be revealed reading downward.

_ ARM	CLE_	LE_T	◯
M_LE	_OTA	_NCH	◯
LAI_	C_OP	DA_E	◯
BE_T	_LUG	MOS_	◯
CI_Y	_OOK	A_OM	◯

Couplets

The picture is of a central circle surrounded by shapes, linked to form six sets of three shapes apiece. Can you complete the puzzle by placing each of the two-letter groups below, one per shape, so that every set of three (the central circle, plus the two matching shapes diagonally opposite one another) forms a six-letter word?

Whichever pair of letters you place in the central circle will appear in the middle of every word.

BE

CA

DE

ES

LE

LL

VA

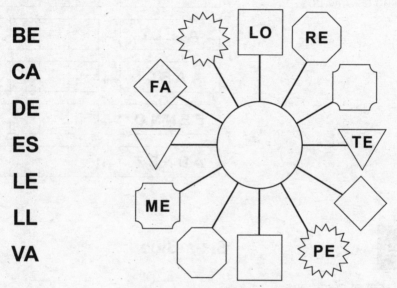

Magic Square

Three letters are already in place in this grid. Use the given letters to fill the empty squares, so that the words reading across are exactly the same as those reading down.

A A A D D

E E E E E H

M M N N S

S S S S T T

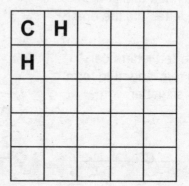

Drop Out

The letters to the left belong in the squares immediately to the right, but not necessarily in the given order. When entered correctly, they reveal the names of five composers, reading downwards.

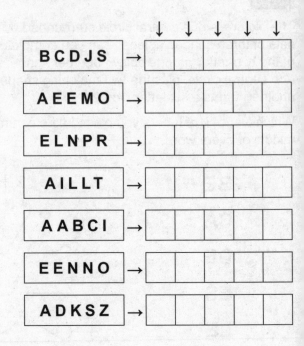

	B C D J S →					
	A E E M O →					
	E L N P R →					
	A I L L T →					
	A A B C I →					
	E E N N O →					
	A D K S Z →					

Six-a-Side

Each set of hexagons contains a six-letter word, reading around the central number in a clockwise direction.

Each word begins with the letter in the shaded square, and you need to place the missing letter into the empty hexagon.

The inserted letters can then be rearranged to form another six-letter word.

Answer:

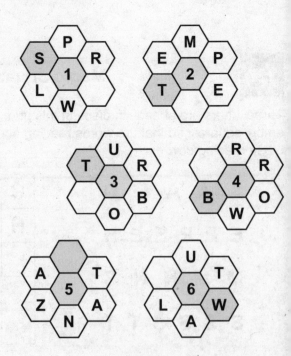

A Novel Approach

Answer the clues by using the groups of letters in the lower box, crossing them out as you go, and placing one letter per square into the grid.

When finished, the remaining letters can be rearranged to make the title of a novel by the author revealed reading down the shaded column.

1 Occurring at fixed intervals

2 Small guitar with four strings

3 Needing a drink

4 Truthfulness

5 Gioacchino ___, composer

6 Went in

7 Nine-sided figure

8 Precious gem

9 Stylish, graceful

10 Salad vegetable

11 16th president of the USA

Novel: _____

ON	CE	HO	EGA	EFA	LI	LE	SI
EN	CE	RE	ULE	MO	ROS	OF	LET
ESP	THI	TE	TY	TY	GU	NT	NO
NES	ND	NI	TH	TU	RS	RED	ASS
OLN	UK	EL	TR	NAG	NC	LAR	DIA

The Bottom Line

Can you fill each square in the bottom line with the correct letter, to make a four-letter word?

Every square in the solution contains only one letter from each of the numbered lines above, although two or more squares in the solution may contain the same letter.

At the end of every line is a score, which shows:

a the number of letters placed in the correct finishing position on the bottom line; and

b the number of letters that appear on the bottom line, but in a different position.

					Correctly Placed	Incorrectly Placed
1	A	R	C	H	0	2
2	B	U	S	R	0	2
3	E	H	U	A	0	2
4	R	C	B	S	0	2
5	A	S	H	E	0	2
					4	0

Words Apart

Use the groups of letters on the right to complete the nine-letter words in each row, writing one letter into each square in the order in which they appear. All groups must be used. When the grid is correctly filled, reading down the shaded columns will spell out a two-word phrase.

						E	R	T
						N	C	Y
						E	N	T
						U	N	D
						A	S	E
						O	U	S
						I	N	G
						T	E	S

COR	QUE
SCI	EXT
BRI	BFO
ROV	UNT
OBY	CON
FRE	DUM
PUL	KIL
FLA	EFC

Downwords

The answers to the clues are all nine-letter words, the letters of which are contained in the grid below, at the rate of one per row in the correct order. Every square is used once only.

1 Entertainment venue

2 Military strength

3 Ballet position

4 South American country

5 Game played with a shuttlecock

6 Word that qualifies a noun

7 Rodent catcher

8 Device used to open bottles

9 Former name of Ethiopia

A	A	A	B	C	F	M	N	V
A	B	D	E	I	I	O	O	R
A	D	G	J	N	R	R	U	Y
B	E	E	E	H	K	M	S	S
C	E	E	I	P	S	S	T	Z
C	C	I	N	O	S	T	T	U
E	I	L	N	Q	R	R	T	W
A	E	E	I	L	O	U	U	V
A	A	B	E	E	N	P	R	W

134

Alphabet Soup

Fill each of the empty squares of this grid with a different letter of the alphabet. Cross off the letters below as you use them.

135

Out of Place

Place all of the missing letters into the grid, one letter in each empty square to create words that read across and down. Every letter must be placed somewhere within the row or column against which it appears.

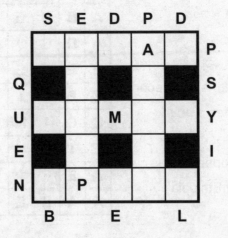

Step by Step

When the seven listed girls' names are correctly placed in the horizontal rows, one letter per square, another girl's name will be revealed reading down the highlighted steps top left to bottom right. Some letters are already in place.

ABIGAIL   **MADONNA**

ANNABEL   **NATALIE**

JESSICA   **YOLANDE**

LETITIA

						I	
A							
							E
	E						

Three Down

Fit six of the nine listed words into the horizontal rows in the grid, so that the remaining three words read down the shaded columns.

ANTICS   **GLOSSY**   **QUARTO**
ATRIUM   **OCCURS**   **SPRANG**
CARTEL   **PAUNCH**   **WHIMSY**

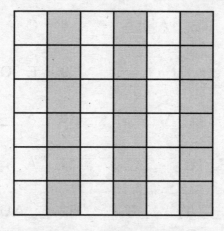

Pyragram

The answer on each level of the pyramid is a single word that is an anagram of the letters in the clue to the left. Place one letter per square in order to reveal the word reading down the shaded column.

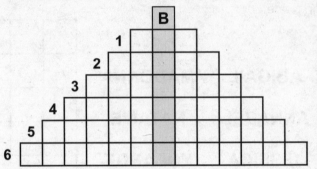

1 Wed
2 Lemon
3 Abridge
4 I am on a bet
5 Curtail urge
6 Mop my clarinet

Consonant Hunt

Twelve names of Roman emperors have had their consonants removed; can you put them all back in their proper places?

Use each of the given letters once only.

**B B C C C C D D D G G G H J L L L
L L M N N N N N N P R R R R S S S
S S S S S T T T T T T T T T**

1 _ A _ _ I A _   7 _ _ A _ A _

2 _ I O _ _ E _ I A _   8 _ O _ _ U _ U _

3 A U _ U _ _ U _   9 _ E _ O

4 _ A _ I _ U _ A   10 _ A _ _ A

5 _ I _ E _ I U _   11 _ A _ I _ U _

6 _ O _ _ _ A _ _ I _ E   12 _ _ A U _ I U _

Alphafill

Place 25 different letters of the alphabet, one per circle, in order to spell out the listed words. Words are formed by moving between adjacent circles along the connecting lines, either horizontally, vertically, or diagonally in any direction.

Begin by crossing out the letters already in place, together with the one letter that doesn't appear in any of the words.

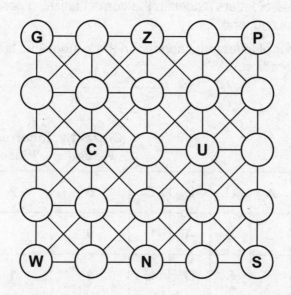

A B C D E F G H I J K L M

N O P Q R S T U V W X Y Z

BEAUTY	JOG	PITY
CREAKY	JULY	QUAVER
DREW	KNAVE	SLAVE
EXULT	LACE	WEAK
FORE	MIXER	ZIP

The Bottom Line

Can you fill each square in the bottom line with the correct letter, to make a four-letter word?

Every square in the solution contains only one letter from each of the numbered lines above, although two or more squares in the solution may contain the same letter.

At the end of every line is a score, which shows:

a the number of letters placed in the correct finishing position on the bottom line; and

b the number of letters that appear on the bottom line, but in a different position.

					Correctly Placed	Incorrectly Placed
1	A	U	L	D	0	2
2	O	S	A	U	0	1
3	I	S	D	U	1	1
4	S	I	O	E	0	2
5	O	L	I	A	1	1
					4	0

Word Ladder

Change one letter at a time (but not the position of any letter) to make a new word – and move from the word at the top of the ladder to the word at the bottom using the exact number of rungs provided.

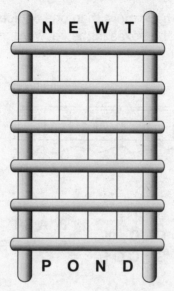

N E W T

P O N D

Word Wheel

Using the letters in the wheel, you have ten minutes to find as many words as possible of three or more letters, none of which may be plurals, foreign words or proper nouns.

Each word must contain the central letter and no letters can be used more than once per word unless they appear in different sections of the wheel.

There is at least one nine-letter word to be found.

Nine-letter word(s):

_____

144   Keyword

On the face of it, this puzzle is perfectly straightforward. Simply fill in the letters missing from words 1-10 and enter them into the numbered boxes, to reveal the hidden keyword.

However, it's possible to have more than one choice of letter for many of the words, so don't fill in the boxes in the keyword until you are quite sure!

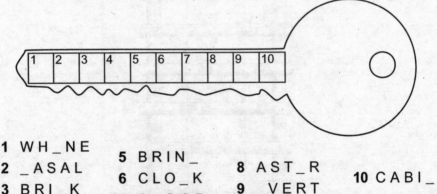

| 1 | 2 | 3 | 4 | 5 | 6 | 7 | 8 | 9 | 10 |

1 WH _ NE

2 _ ASAL

3 BRI _ K

4 A _ ART

5 BRIN _

6 CLO _ K

7 S _ OOD

8 AST _ R

9 _ VERT

10 CABI _

145   On the Tiles

Fit the eight tiles into the pattern, to form four words reading across and five words reading down. No tile may be rotated.

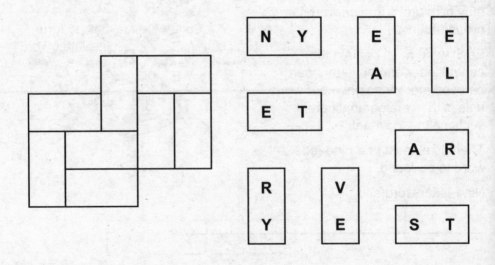

Missing Vowels

All the vowels in this crossword have been removed. Can you replace them, using exactly the quantity shown below?

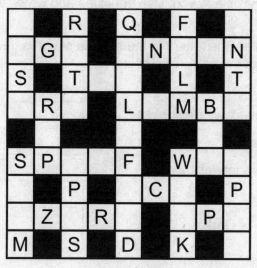

A A A A A
E E E E E E E E
I I I I I
O O O O O O O O
U U

Nine Threes

Using the given letters once only, place one into each empty box, to form nine three-letter words reading down the columns, and one nine-letter word reading across the central row.

E H I N O P R S W

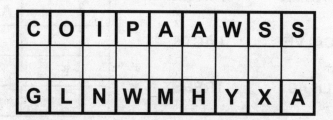

148   Dice Section

Printed onto every one of the six numbered dice are six letters (one per face), that can be rearranged to form the answer to each clue; however, some sides are invisible to you. Use the clues and write every answer into the grid.

When correctly filled, the letters in the shaded squares, reading in the order 1 to 6, will spell out the name of a country.

1 Short-lived, winged insect

2 Keg, cask

3 Italian variety of sausage

4 Revoke

5 Capital of Oman

6 Talks

149   Red Herring

Five of the words below must be entered in the grid, reading across, so as to create five more words reading down. Two letters are already in place. Can you spot the red herring?

AROMA   NEVER

CALVE   PACTS

LILAC   TRESS

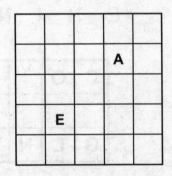

Three, Four, Ten

Place each group of three letters into the shaded squares, keeping their letters in order, so that three four-letter words are formed in each row.

Some groups of letters will fit into more than one place, but only the correct combination will lead to four ten-letter words reading down the columns topped by a star.

			☆	☆					☆	☆	
G	A	R				A	Y	F			
S	A	R				S	T	U			
D	A	W				R	Y	M			
D	A	D				R	Y	S			
Z	I	N				E	X	O			
E	C	R				O	W	P			
B	A	W				L	M	O			
F	L	E				U	T	P			
E	W	E				S	K	S			
A	L	A				O	W	L			

- ALT
- APA
- ASC
- BBR
- CIB
- EWD
- GRE
- IBE
- IRM
- LFI
- NDO
- NSP
- OBU
- RAL
- RTA
- SSN
- TUN
- UCH
- UFL
- URR

The Bottom Line

Can you fill each square in the bottom line with the correct letter, to make a four-letter word?

Every square in the solution contains only one letter from each of the numbered lines above, although two or more squares in the solution may contain the same letter.

At the end of every line is a score, which shows:

a the number of letters placed in the correct finishing position on the bottom line; and

b the number of letters that appear on the bottom line, but in a different position.

					Correctly Placed	Incorrectly Placed
1	U	M	B	O	0	2
2	E	R	G	U	0	1
3	M	U	G	B	1	1
4	M	O	P	G	0	2
5	B	P	E	M	0	2
					4	0

Egg Timer

Can you complete this puzzle in the time it takes to boil an egg?

The answers to the clues are anagrams of the words immediately above and below, plus or minus one letter.

1 Lured, cajoled

2 Fraudulence

3 Decree, proclamation

4 Secured with a rope

5 Lukewarm

6 Portray

7 Forecast

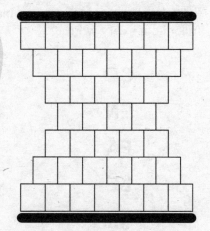

Holesome Fun

In this puzzle, you must find a five-letter word by deciding which common letter has been removed from the trios of words. Place that letter into the hole at the end of each row and the answer will be revealed reading downward.

O _ A L	_ A I L	C L I _	◯
D I _ L	C O L _	S T _ Y	◯
_ I S K	C U _ L	_ E A D	◯
G O A _	_ H E N	L A _ E	◯
L _ R E	V E R _	_ O K E	◯

Couplets

The picture is of a central circle surrounded by shapes, linked to form six sets of three shapes apiece. Can you complete the puzzle by placing each of the two-letter groups below, one per shape, so that every set of three (the central circle, plus the two matching shapes diagonally opposite one another) forms a six-letter word?

Whichever pair of letters you place in the central circle will appear in the middle of every word.

CO

EN

FA

LE

MI

RE

SE

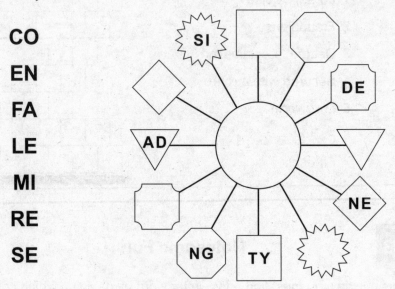

Magic Square

Three letters are already in place in this grid. Use the given letters to fill the empty squares, so that the words reading across are exactly the same as those reading down.

B B C E E

E E G G N N

O O O O R

R R R S S T

156

Drop Out

The letters to the left belong in the squares immediately to the right, but not necessarily in the given order. When entered correctly, they reveal the names of five languages, reading downwards.

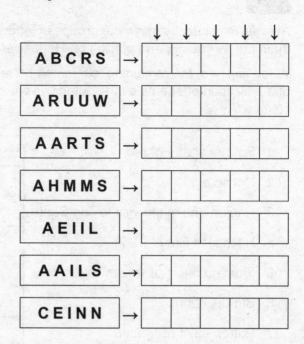

| ABCRS → |
| ARUUW → |
| AARTS → |
| AHMMS → |
| AEIIL → |
| AAILS → |
| CEINN → |

157

Six-a-Side

Each set of hexagons contains a six-letter word, reading around the central number in a clockwise direction.

Each word begins with the letter in the shaded square, and you need to place the missing letter into the empty hexagon.

The inserted letters can then be rearranged to form another six-letter word.

Answer:

_____

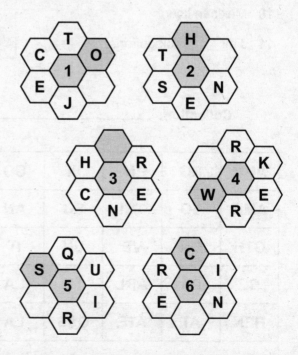

A Novel Approach

Answer the clues by using the groups of letters in the lower box, crossing them out as you go, and placing one letter per square into the grid.

When finished, the remaining letters can be rearranged to make the title of a collection of poems by the author revealed reading down the shaded column.

1 Brilliant shade of red

2 Not so old

3 Region one might visit to see Santa

4 Hitchcock film of 1958

5 Floating mass of frozen water

6 Stir up, churn

7 Patron saint of Ireland

8 Country, capital Beirut

9 US state, capital Montgomery

10 Mexican liquor

11 Jimi ___, rock guitarist

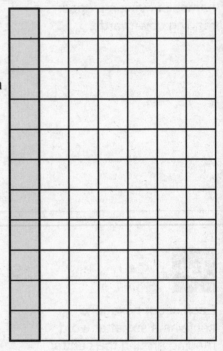

Collection: _____

AND	RG	IN	IX	GO	AG	AL	CR
AMA	YO	TRI	SC	AN	ER	PL	DR
GTH	ON	VE	UN	IT	RTI	AB	ICE
BE	PA	ARL	TE	LA	LEB	EW	QUI
HEN	AT	ATE	OSS	LA	GER	CK	ET

The Bottom Line

Can you fill each square in the bottom line with the correct letter, to make a four-letter word?

Every square in the solution contains only one letter from each of the numbered lines above, although two or more squares in the solution may contain the same letter.

At the end of every line is a score, which shows:

a   the number of letters placed in the correct finishing position on the bottom line; and

b   the number of letters that appear on the bottom line, but in a different position.

					Correctly Placed	Incorrectly Placed
1	K	N	I	T	1	1
2	C	O	F	I	1	1
3	G	T	K	C	1	1
4	F	K	O	T	1	1
5	N	G	F	O	1	1
					4	0

Words Apart

Use the groups of letters on the right to complete the nine-letter words in each row, writing one letter into each square in the order in which they appear. All groups must be used. When the grid is correctly filled, reading down the shaded columns will spell out a two-word phrase.

						I	S	E
						U	N	D
						I	N	G
						E	A	R
						D	E	D
						A	N	D
						L	I	C
						O	M	E

REC	**DST**
VEL	**SCR**
HAN	**TRU**
IMP	**DEE**
NGE	**EVA**
PRO	**DIS**
RHO	**ODR**
EAM	**APP**

Downwords

The answers to the clues are all nine-letter words, the letters of which are contained in the grid below, at the rate of one per row in the correct order. Every square is used once only.

1 What is left

2 Having the capacity to soak up liquids

3 Study of the Earth's surface

4 Vellum

5 City in Israel

6 Arm of the Atlantic Ocean

7 Get rid of, completely remove

8 Subsequently

9 Country, capital Vilnius

A	A	C	E	G	J	L	P	R
A	A	B	E	E	E	F	I	L
I	M	O	R	R	R	S	T	T
A	C	E	G	H	I	M	O	U
B	H	I	I	R	R	R	S	U
A	A	A	B	B	M	N	N	W
A	A	D	E	E	E	L	N	P
A	E	E	H	I	N	N	R	T
A	D	E	M	N	R	T	T	Y

Alphabet Soup

Fill each of the empty squares of this grid with a different letter of the alphabet. Cross off the letters below as you use them.

Letters (left column): A B C D E F G H I J K L M

Letters (right column): N O P Q R S T U V W X Y Z

Grid (row labels A–M):

A		A	L	S	E			R	O	W	
B	A					U		B		A	
C	T	R	A			R			A	W	
D	E		P		A		R	E			
E				N				C		E	
F											
G			U	I			U	T	O		
H	O		N		H						
I	N			L	V	E			V		
J	A	D		A		S	T	O		E	
K	T		O					N			
L											
M	A	N		L	E	S		E	E	T	

Out of Place

Place all of the missing letters into the grid, one letter in each empty square to create words that read across and down. Every letter must be placed somewhere within the row or column against which it appears.

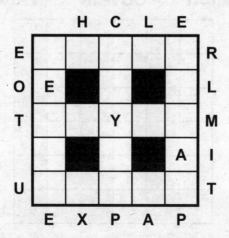

Top letters: H C L E

Left column labels (top to bottom): E O T U

Right column labels (top to bottom): R L M I T

Bottom letters: E X P A P

103

164   Step by Step

When the seven listed words are correctly placed in the horizontal rows, one letter per square, two more words will be revealed reading down the highlighted steps top left to bottom right, and top right to bottom left. Some letters are already in place.

BRAVERY   IMPRESS

CHAPTER   PLATOON

CULTURE   SCALLOP

EXHAUST

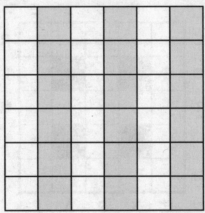

165   Three Down

Fit six of the nine listed words into the horizontal rows in the grid, so that the remaining three words read down the shaded columns.

ABLAZE   JOYFUL   STAMEN
ANCHOR   LENDER   TISSUE
FAMISH   OBTAIN   VARIED

166   Pyragram

The answer on each level of the pyramid is a single word that is an anagram of the letters in the clue to the left. Place one letter per square in order to reveal the word reading down the shaded column.

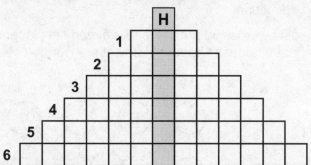

1 Tog

2 Ample

3 Art base

4 A red shift

5 Cadet ritual

6 A document clip

167   Consonant Hunt

Twelve names of artists have had their consonants removed; can you put them all back in their proper places?

Use each of the given letters once only.

**B B B B B C C C C C C D G G G G G G
H H H H L L L L L L L M M N N N N
N N P R R R R R R R R S S S S T T T
T T T T T T T V W**

1 _O_ _I_E_ _I

2 _I_A_ _O

3 _A_ _O_

4 _O_ _ _A_ _E

5 _I_ _O_E_ _O

6 _ _UE_ _E_

7 _I_ _E_A_ _E_O

8 _A_A_A_ _IO

9 _U_ _E_

10 _E_ _ _A_ _ _

11 _A_A_E_ _O

12 _AI_ _ _O_OU_ _

105

Alphafill

Place 25 different letters of the alphabet, one per circle, in order to spell out the listed words. Words are formed by moving between adjacent circles along the connecting lines, either horizontally, vertically, or diagonally in any direction.

Begin by crossing out the letters already in place, together with the one letter that doesn't appear in any of the words.

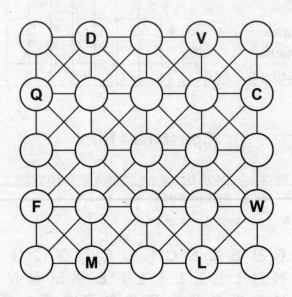

A B C D E F G H I J K L M

N O P Q R S T U V W X Y Z

BAIZE	QUIZ	TAXES
FUND	RUIN	VACANT
JUNTA	SMOKE	WEIRD
MOUNT	SKIN	WHELK
PRINT	SOJOURN	YOKEL

The Bottom Line

Can you fill each square in the bottom line with the correct letter, to make a four-letter word?

Every square in the solution contains only one letter from each of the numbered lines above, although two or more squares in the solution may contain the same letter.

At the end of every line is a score, which shows:

a the number of letters placed in the correct finishing position on the bottom line; and

b the number of letters that appear on the bottom line, but in a different position.

					Correctly Placed	Incorrectly Placed
1	T	U	B	E	1	0
2	B	I	R	O	0	2
3	R	O	I	L	0	2
4	L	L	T	R	0	2
5	O	B	B	I	0	1
					4	0

170   Word Ladder

Change one letter at a time (but not the position of any letter) to make a new word – and move from the word at the top of the ladder to the word at the bottom using the exact number of rungs provided.

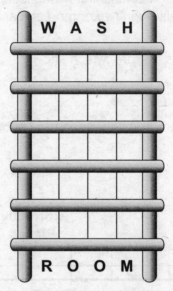

W A S H

R O O M

171   Word Wheel

Using the letters in the wheel, you have ten minutes to find as many words as possible of three or more letters, none of which may be plurals, foreign words or proper nouns.

Each word must contain the central letter and no letters can be used more than once per word unless they appear in different sections of the wheel.

There is at least one nine-letter word to be found.

Nine-letter word(s):

Keyword

On the face of it, this puzzle is perfectly straightforward. Simply fill in the letters missing from words 1-10 and enter them into the numbered boxes, to reveal the hidden keyword.

However, it's possible to have more than one choice of letter for many of the words, so don't fill in the boxes in the keyword until you are quite sure!

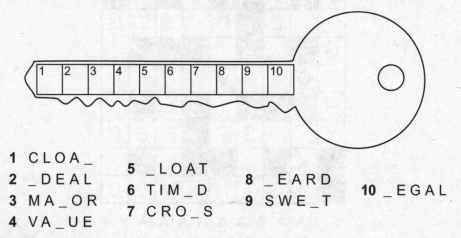

1 CLOA _
2 _ DEAL
3 MA _ OR
4 VA _ UE

5 _ LOAT
6 TIM _ D
7 CRO _ S

8 _ EARD
9 SWE _ T

10 _ EGAL

On the Tiles

Fit the eight tiles into the pattern, to form four words reading across and five words reading down. No tile may be rotated.

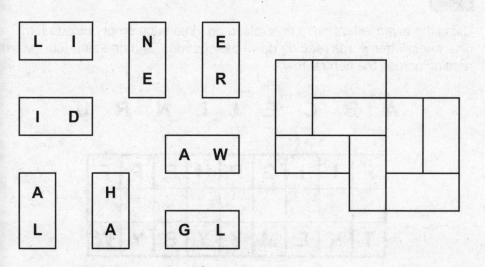

174   Missing Vowels

All the vowels in this crossword have been removed. Can you replace them, using exactly the quantity shown below?

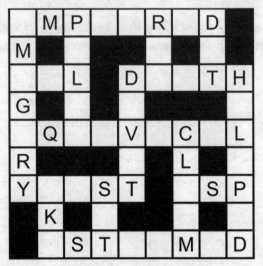

A A A A A A A A A

E E E E E E E E E E

I I I I I I I

O O

U U U

175   Nine Threes

Using the given letters once only, place one into each empty box, to form nine three-letter words reading down the columns, and one nine-letter word reading across the central row.

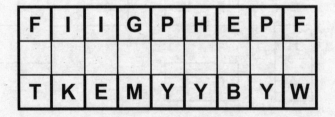

A   B   C   E   I   L   N   R   U

F	I	I	G	P	H	E	P	F
T	K	E	M	Y	Y	B	Y	W

Dice Section

Printed onto every one of the six numbered dice are six letters (one per face), that can be rearranged to form the answer to each clue; however, some sides are invisible to you. Use the clues and write every answer into the grid.

When correctly filled, the letters in the shaded squares, reading in the order 1 to 6, will spell out the name of a composer.

1 Blossom, bloom

2 Beaded counting frame

3 Mythical fire-breather

4 Landing strip

5 Most uncommon

6 Orange root vegetable

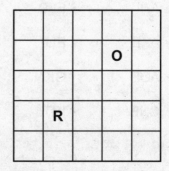

Red Herring

Five of the words below must be entered in the grid, reading across, so as to create five more words reading down. Two letters are already in place. Can you spot the red herring?

ALPHA   SOLOS

ERASE   SPACE

RESET   TIERS

Three, Four, Ten

Place each group of three letters into the shaded squares, keeping their letters in order, so that three four-letter words are formed in each row.

Some groups of letters will fit into more than one place, but only the correct combination will lead to four ten-letter words reading down the columns topped by a star.

			☆	☆				☆	☆	
L	A	M			E	Y	F			
C	O	R			A	Y	A			
A	B	E			R	K	E			
T	U	N			N	T	U			
F	R	O			E	W	B			
U	N	D			R	Y	S			
C	Y	A			O	K	S			
Y	E	T			I	M	D			
B	O	S			L	T	A			
W	H	A			U	E	W			

- AHI
- AKE
- AOB
- CNE
- ELD
- ELL
- GKN
- IRT
- ISW
- NAP
- NBO
- NBR
- OSP
- PEX
- PIC
- RDU
- SPE
- TBA
- TOA
- TTR

The Bottom Line

Can you fill each square in the bottom line with the correct letter, to make a four-letter word?

Every square in the solution contains only one letter from each of the numbered lines above, although two or more squares in the solution may contain the same letter.

At the end of every line is a score, which shows:

a the number of letters placed in the correct finishing position on the bottom line; and

b the number of letters that appear on the bottom line, but in a different position.

					Correctly Placed	Incorrectly Placed
1	S	I	F	T	1	1
2	F	T	A	O	1	1
3	T	F	E	P	1	1
4	F	S	A	P	1	1
5	T	I	E	O	0	2
					4	0

180 Egg Timer

Can you complete this puzzle in the time it takes to boil an egg?

The answers to the clues are anagrams of the words immediately above and below, plus or minus one letter.

1 Inhabitant of the
   Red Planet?
2 Capital of Albania
3 Rail-based transport
4 Muslim country
5 Organ of the central
   nervous system
6 Sash
7 Bandit

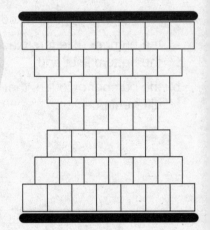

181 Holesome Fun

In this puzzle, you must find a five-letter word by deciding which common letter has been removed from the trios of words. Place that letter into the hole at the end of each row and the answer will be revealed reading downward.

LI _ E	_ O T E	A _ I D	◯
C _ K E	S _ I L	Y O G _	◯
_ I M E	B E L _	C _ O G	◯
W _ L T	M _ C E	C L _ P	◯
B O _ Y	W A R _	_ I A L	◯

Couplets

The picture is of a central circle surrounded by shapes, linked to form six sets of three shapes apiece. Can you complete the puzzle by placing each of the two-letter groups below, one per shape, so that every set of three (the central circle, plus the two matching shapes diagonally opposite one another) forms a six-letter word?

Whichever pair of letters you place in the central circle will appear in the middle of every word.

AS
CO
EC
HO
LD
OL
UN

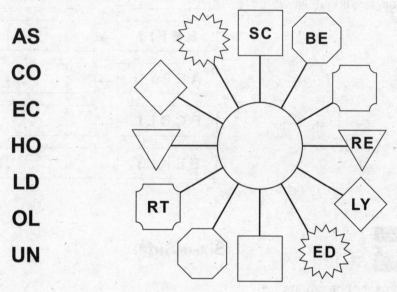

183   Magic Square

Three letters are already in place in this grid. Use the given letters to fill the empty squares, so that the words reading across are exactly the same as those reading down.

C C D E E

E E F H H I

I M N O O

R R R R T T

C	A			
A				

184

Drop Out

The letters to the left belong in the squares immediately to the right, but not necessarily in the given order. When entered correctly, they reveal the names of five Beatles songs, reading downwards.

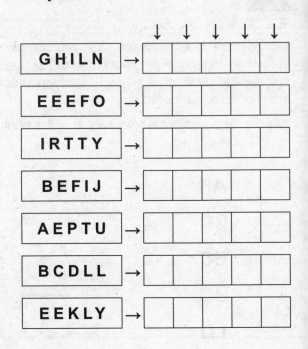

185

Six-a-Side

Each set of hexagons contains a six-letter word, reading around the central number in a clockwise direction.

Each word begins with the letter in the shaded square, and you need to place the missing letter into the empty hexagon.

The inserted letters can then be rearranged to form another six-letter word.

Answer:

_____

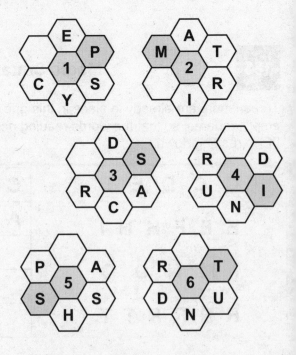

A Novel Approach

Answer the clues by using the groups of letters in the lower box, crossing them out as you go, and placing one letter per square into the grid.

When finished, the remaining letters can be rearranged to make the title of a novel by the author revealed reading down the shaded column.

1 Country, capital Rabat

2 Circus performer

3 Take delivery of

4 Mexican state, capital Mérida

5 Compress

6 Harry ____, escape artist

7 Raise to a higher position

8 Not as heavy

9 Acquired knowledge

10 Investigate

11 Gave way

Novel: _____

	AN	ZE	CAT	AT	EX	OC	
ER	AN	TH	EL	EVA	EE	YI	LI
CO	HO	EL	ROB	RN	EL	UD	ORE
ED	AS	GHT	INI	SQU	YU	LEA	VE
CEI	DED	RE	PL	MOR	TM	TE	AC

The Bottom Line

Can you fill each square in the bottom line with the correct letter, to make a four-letter word?

Every square in the solution contains only one letter from each of the numbered lines above, although two or more squares in the solution may contain the same letter.

At the end of every line is a score, which shows:

a the number of letters placed in the correct finishing position on the bottom line; and

b the number of letters that appear on the bottom line, but in a different position.

					Correctly Placed	Incorrectly Placed
1	A	D	I	T	0	2
2	D	E	F	T	1	1
3	E	I	O	F	1	1
4	N	I	O	A	1	1
5	O	D	E	A	0	2
					4	0

Words Apart

Use the groups of letters on the right to complete the nine-letter words in each row, writing one letter into each square in the order in which they appear. All groups must be used. When the grid is correctly filled, reading down the shaded columns will spell out a two-word phrase.

						I	O	N
						P	E	D
						D	I	C
						T	E	R
						I	N	G
						O	U	S
						A	T	E
						H	T	S

AME	**ORI**
ENT	**ORK**
CUL	**ESS**
UNC	**LIG**
MIN	**PAR**
RAP	**NOT**
OBS	**RAI**
NWA	**SKY**

Downwords

The answers to the clues are all nine-letter words, the letters of which are contained in the grid below, at the rate of one per row in the correct order. Every square is used once only.

1 Not shared with others

2 Wealth

3 Extremely pleasing to taste

4 Meat-eating animal

5 26th president of the USA

6 Result of learning and reasoning

7 Farm animals, generally

8 Brilliant red, scarlet

9 Discuss terms of an arrangement

A	C	D	E	K	L	N	R	V
A	E	E	E	F	I	N	O	X
C	F	L	G	O	O	R	R	V
E	I	L	L	M	N	O	S	W
C	E	I	I	L	S	T	U	U
E	E	I	I	L	S	T	V	V
A	D	E	I	I	N	O	O	O
C	C	G	L	O	R	T	U	V
E	E	E	E	E	K	N	S	T

Alphabet Soup

Fill each of the empty squares of this grid with a different letter of the alphabet. Cross off the letters below as you use them.

A		N
B		O
C		P
D		Q
E		R
F		S
G		T
H		U
I		V
J		W
K		X
L		Y
M		Z

Grid:

E			I	P	▮		▮	B		U
	▮	N		L	A	D	I	N		
C	O		R	A		U				L
	▮	A		N	O		E	L	T	
T		I	N		L	E	▮			
E		▮			D	▮		R		W
▮			R	E		R	E	S		
	O	N		U		E	▮	B		E
H	▮	I		M			W		K	E
O	M		I		U			R	▮	
P	▮	E		A			A	N	G	Y

Out of Place

Place all of the missing letters into the grid, one letter in each empty square to create words that read across and down. Every letter must be placed somewhere within the row or column against which it appears.

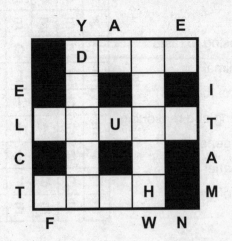

192   Step by Step

When the seven listed words are correctly placed in the horizontal rows, one letter per square, two more words will be revealed reading down the highlighted steps top left to bottom right, and top right to bottom left. Some letters are already in place.

BATTERY   **ROYALTY**

DENMARK   **SCHOOLS**

LACTOSE   **VANILLA**

PIQUANT

193   Three Down

Fit six of the nine listed words into the horizontal rows in the grid, so that the remaining three words read down the shaded columns.

CREDIT	FABLED	REGENT
DEMEAN	GRILLE	SURFER
ESCAPE	HUMBUG	USURER

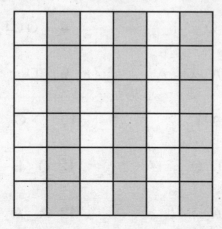

194 — Pyragram

The answer on each level of the pyramid is a single word that is an anagram of the letters in the clue to the left. Place one letter per square in order to reveal the word reading down the shaded column.

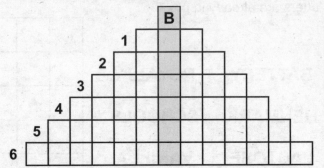

1 Lea
2 Bogle
3 Lattice
4 I, of course
5 Shopper's rag
6 Yacht boarders

195 — Consonant Hunt

Twelve names of US states have had their consonants removed; can you put them all back in their proper places?

Use each of the given letters once only.

B C C F G G H H K K K K L L L

M M M N N N N N N N N R R S S

S S S S T T T W W X Y Y

1 _ E _ _ U _ _ _

2 _ I _ _ O _ _ I _

3 O _ _ A _ O _ A

4 _ A _ A I I

5 _ A _ I _ O _ _ I A

6 _ E _ A _

7 _ E _ _ A _ _ A

8 _ O U I _ I A _ A

9 _ O _ _ A _ A

10 _ _ O _ I _ _

11 O _ E _ O _

12 A _ A _ _ A

122

Alphafill

Place 25 different letters of the alphabet, one per circle, in order to spell out the listed words. Words are formed by moving between adjacent circles along the connecting lines, either horizontally, vertically, or diagonally in any direction.

Begin by crossing out the letters already in place, together with the one letter that doesn't appear in any of the words.

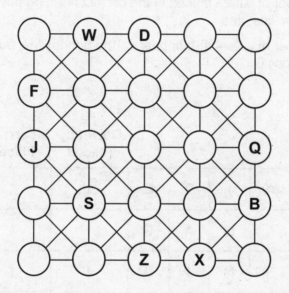

A B C D E F G H I J K L M

N O P Q R S T U V W X Y Z

AXES	JIVES	SHIVERY
BRAVERY	LISP	SILVER
BROWN	MORE	SPEAK
CHILD	OVER	TURQUOISE
FLOUT	REVISE	ZERO

The Bottom Line

Can you fill each square in the bottom line with the correct letter, to make a four-letter word?

Every square in the solution contains only one letter from each of the numbered lines above, although two or more squares in the solution may contain the same letter.

At the end of every line is a score, which shows:

a the number of letters placed in the correct finishing position on the bottom line; and

b the number of letters that appear on the bottom line, but in a different position.

					Correctly Placed	Incorrectly Placed
1	A	I	D	E	1	1
2	N	O	A	G	1	1
3	S	N	I	D	1	1
4	G	S	I	A	1	1
5	E	N	D	O	1	1
					4	0

198 Word Ladder

Change one letter at a time (but not the position of any letter) to make a new word – and move from the word at the top of the ladder to the word at the bottom using the exact number of rungs provided.

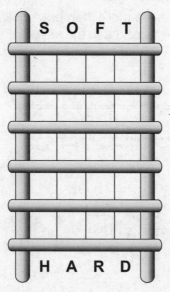

S O F T

H A R D

199 Word Wheel

Using the letters in the wheel, you have ten minutes to find as many words as possible of three or more letters, none of which may be plurals, foreign words or proper nouns.

Each word must contain the central letter and no letters can be used more than once per word unless they appear in different sections of the wheel.

There is at least one nine-letter word to be found.

Nine-letter word(s):

_____

Keyword

On the face of it, this puzzle is perfectly straightforward. Simply fill in the letters missing from words 1-10 and enter them into the numbered boxes, to reveal the hidden keyword.

However, it's possible to have more than one choice of letter for many of the words, so don't fill in the boxes in the keyword until you are quite sure!

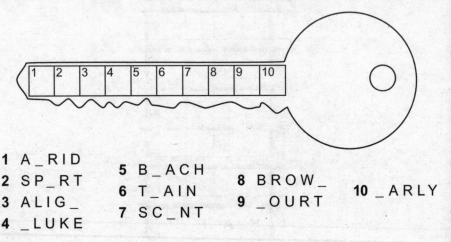

| 1 | 2 | 3 | 4 | 5 | 6 | 7 | 8 | 9 | 10 |

1 A _ R I D
2 S P _ R T
3 A L I G _
4 _ L U K E

5 B _ A C H
6 T _ A I N
7 S C _ N T

8 B R O W _
9 _ O U R T

10 _ A R L Y

On the Tiles

Fit the eight tiles into the pattern, to form four words reading across and five words reading down. No tile may be rotated.

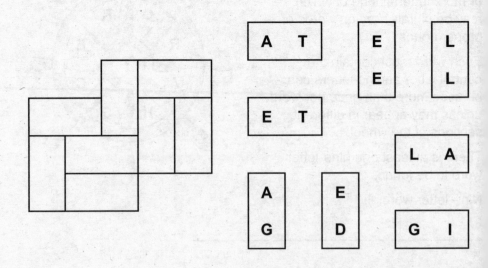

Missing Vowels

All the vowels in this crossword have been removed. Can you replace them, using exactly the quantity shown below?

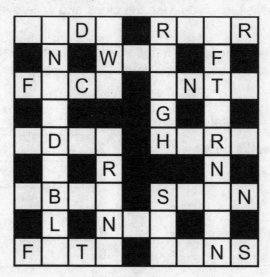

A A A A A

E E E E E E E E E E

I I I I

O O O O O O O O O O

U U

Nine Threes

Using the given letters once only, place one into each empty box, to form nine three-letter words reading down the columns, and one nine-letter word reading across the central row.

E G H I O R S T V

B	I	F	F	A	F	E	W	A
A	Y	Z	Y	P	X	G	O	E

Dice Section

Printed onto every one of the six numbered dice are six letters (one per face), that can be rearranged to form the answer to each clue; however, some sides are invisible to you. Use the clues and write every answer into the grid.

When correctly filled, the letters in the shaded squares, reading in the order 1 to 6, will spell out the name of an item of sports equipment.

1 Country, capital Amman

2 Woodworking tool

3 Child of an aunt or uncle

4 Pail

5 Subtract

6 Ant or beetle, for example

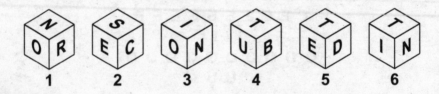

204

Red Herring

205

Five of the words below must be entered in the grid, reading across, so as to create five more words reading down. Two letters are already in place. Can you spot the red herring?

AVOID　　GLARE

DENSE　　MOIST

EDGED　　ROMAN

Three, Four, Ten

Place each group of three letters into the shaded squares, keeping their letters in order, so that three four-letter words are formed in each row.

Some groups of letters will fit into more than one place, but only the correct combination will lead to four ten-letter words reading down the columns topped by a star.

☆		☆				☆		☆
S	A	R				R	B	A			
F	I	L				U	G	Y			
D	U	M				V	Y	W			
H	A	L				E	W	B			
L	I	A				Z	Z	W			
C	Y	S				C	K	O			
C	O	M				I	M	I			
L	A	W				S	P	L			
Z	I	N				Y	E	U			
B	L	U				C	K	U			

- ABR
- ERG
- ILL
- OBL
- RFI
- CST
- FAR
- MSM
- OGI
- RGE
- EDE
- GLE
- NCA
- PLE
- SER
- END
- IBA
- NGA
- REN
- TRO

The Bottom Line

Can you fill each square in the bottom line with the correct letter, to make a four-letter word?

Every square in the solution contains only one letter from each of the numbered lines above, although two or more squares in the solution may contain the same letter.

At the end of every line is a score, which shows:

a the number of letters placed in the correct finishing position on the bottom line; and

b the number of letters that appear on the bottom line, but in a different position.

					Correctly Placed	Incorrectly Placed
1	A	R	C	S	0	2
2	E	F	T	A	0	2
3	T	E	A	C	0	2
4	R	C	E	L	0	2
5	T	C	S	F	1	1
					4	0

Egg Timer

Can you complete this puzzle in the time it takes to boil an egg?

The answers to the clues are anagrams of the words immediately above and below, plus or minus one letter.

1 Short period of rest or relief
2 Man of God
3 Animal's stomach used as food
4 Cheeky, irreverent
5 Come to a point
6 Catch, capture
7 Black leopard

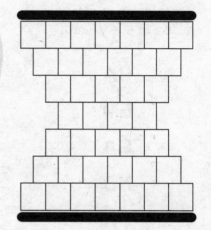

Holesome Fun

In this puzzle, you must find a five-letter word by deciding which common letter has been removed from the trios of words. Place that letter into the hole at the end of each row and the answer will be revealed reading downward.

PE_K	_OAL	A_RE	◯
_ING	T_UE	DEE_	◯
M_ST	_LSO	LE_N	◯
S_UG	BEA_	_EXT	◯
DIN_	IT_M	_DIT	◯

Couplets

The picture is of a central circle surrounded by shapes, linked to form six sets of three shapes apiece. Can you complete the puzzle by placing each of the two-letter groups below, one per shape, so that every set of three (the central circle, plus the two matching shapes diagonally opposite one another) forms a six-letter word?

Whichever pair of letters you place in the central circle will appear in the middle of every word.

BA

EM

GA

ND

OR

RA

SU

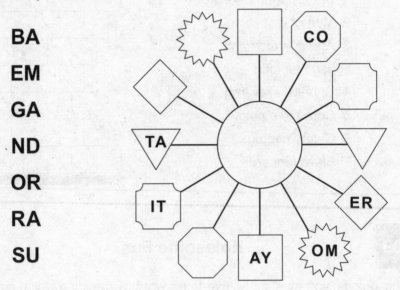

Magic Square

Three letters are already in place in this grid. Use the given letters to fill the empty squares, so that the words reading across are exactly the same as those reading down.

B B E E E

E G G H H I

I I I L N

N O T T T T

Drop Out

The letters to the left belong in the squares immediately to the right, but not necessarily in the given order. When entered correctly, they reveal the names of five breeds of dog, reading downwards.

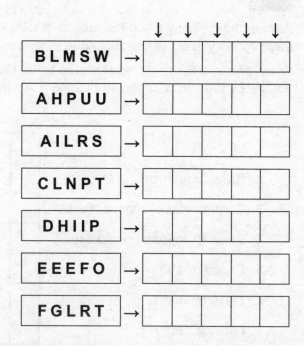

		↓	↓	↓	↓	↓
B L M S W	→					
A H P U U	→					
A I L R S	→					
C L N P T	→					
D H I I P	→					
E E E F O	→					
F G L R T	→					

213

Six-a-Side

Each set of hexagons contains a six-letter word, reading around the central number in a clockwise direction.

Each word begins with the letter in the shaded square, and you need to place the missing letter into the empty hexagon.

The inserted letters can then be rearranged to form another six-letter word.

Answer:

_____

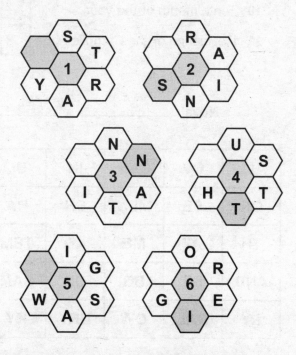

A Novel Approach

Answer the clues by using the groups of letters in the lower box, crossing them out as you go, and placing one letter per square into the grid.

When finished, the remaining letters can be rearranged to make the title of a novel by the author revealed reading down the shaded column.

1 Vast

2 Russian tea urn

3 Commander of a naval fleet

4 Small European principality

5 Period of 100 years

6 Make an effort

7 Lacking depth

8 Whim

9 Nearest planet to the Sun

10 Tenth month of the year

11 Residence of the Catholic Pope

Novel: _____

ALL	OV	CAN	IN	UL	MI	VA	ES
OR	SE	MEN	SH	RA	PE	IMP	NT
TH	AT	ME	AD	TEM	RCU	IM	OCT
AND	SE	BB	OB	SAM	CE	PT	AR
RY	RAL	OW	URY	KY	ER	LE	TI

215 — The Bottom Line

Can you fill each square in the bottom line with the correct letter, to make a five-letter word?

Every square in the solution contains only one letter from each of the numbered lines above, although two or more squares in the solution may contain the same letter.

At the end of every line is a score, which shows:

a the number of letters placed in the correct finishing position on the bottom line; and

b the number of letters that appear on the bottom line, but in a different position.

						Correctly Placed	Incorrectly Placed
1	R	E	M	I	T	0	1
2	A	R	E	H	U	1	1
3	A	U	T	G	I	0	2
4	M	U	M	I	S	1	0
5	I	E	I	E	S	1	0
6	H	E	M	S	U	1	0
						5	0

135

Words Apart

Use the groups of letters on the right to complete the nine-letter words in each row, writing one letter into each square in the order in which they appear. All groups must be used. When the grid is correctly filled, reading down the shaded columns will spell out a two-word phrase.

						O	L	D
						A	C	Y
						L	L	Y
						O	P	E
						R	I	C
						O	U	S
						I	N	T
						I	U	M

ERI	ICA
HOR	WPO
DEM	IMP
ZIR	BLI
TYP	VIE
MET	OCR
NDF	GEO
CON	OSC

Downwords

The answers to the clues are all nine-letter words, the letters of which are contained in the grid below, at the rate of one per row in the correct order. Every square is used once only.

1 Pouched mammal

2 Vigorous, lively

3 Continent in the southern hemisphere

4 Violent desert phenomenon

5 Flash during a thunderstorm

6 Birthplace of Jesus

7 Significant

8 Having eight sides

9 Shaking

A	B	E	I	L	M	O	S	T
A	A	C	E	I	M	N	R	U
E	E	G	N	P	R	S	T	T
A	D	H	H	M	O	R	S	T
B	G	G	L	R	R	S	T	U
A	E	E	L	N	O	P	T	T
A	H	I	I	I	L	N	O	T
A	A	E	I	I	N	N	N	R
A	C	G	G	L	L	M	M	T

Alphabet Soup

Fill each of the empty squares of this grid with a different letter of the alphabet. Cross off the letters below as you use them.

	A	B	C	D	E	F	G	H	I	J	K	
A	S	A		O		■	B	L		A		**N**
B	I	■	O	■			■	I			O	**O**
C		■		G		■	N	E	C			**P**
D	T	O		A	H	A		K	■		E	**Q**
E	H	■	I		T		A			E	N	**R**
F	■		N			■	T	■	I	■		**S**
G		O	G	M	A		C				C	**T**
H	E	■		A	R			D		K	E	**U**
I	L	A			■			A		D		**V**
J		■			■	U		N		A		**W**
K	E	A		E	R	■	L		T	E		**X**
L												**Y**
M												**Z**

Out of Place

Place all of the missing letters into the grid, one letter in each empty square to create words that read across and down. Every letter must be placed somewhere within the row or column against which it appears.

220

Step by Step

When the seven listed words are correctly placed in the horizontal rows, one letter per square, two more words will be revealed reading down the highlighted steps top left to bottom right, and top right to bottom left. Some letters are already in place.

CAPSULE	RIVALRY
HIRSUTE	SAWMILL
PERPLEX	SETTLER
PSYCHIC	

			C			
						E
S						
			A			

221

Three Down

Fit six of the nine listed words into the horizontal rows in the grid, so that the remaining three words read down the shaded columns.

BOXING	FUSION	RUEFUL
CAVORT	LENGTH	SPOUSE
DRENCH	PRISON	UPROAR

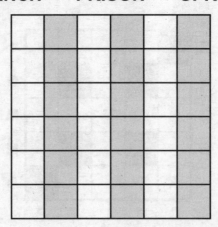

Pyragram

The answer on each level of the pyramid is a single word that is an anagram of the letters in the clue to the left. Place one letter per square in order to reveal the word reading down the shaded column.

1 Mug
2 Thorn
3 Teen pun
4 I need Bill
5 Created lace
6 Transmit radio

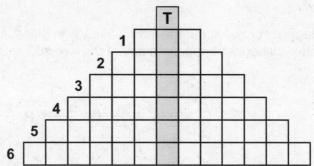

Consonant Hunt

Twelve herbs and spices have had their consonants removed; can you put them all back in their proper places?

Use each of the given letters once only.

B B C C D G G G G G G J K L M M M M
M M M M N N N N N N P P P P P P R R
R R R R R R R R R R R R S S T T T Y Y

1 _O_E_A__

2 _O_A_E

3 _A__O_A_

4 _A__I_A

5 _I__E_

6 _I__A_O_

7 _E__A_O_

8 _E__E__I__

9 O_E_A_O

10 _A___E_

11 _A__A_O_

12 _A__A_O_

Alphafill

Place 25 different letters of the alphabet, one per circle, in order to spell out the listed words. Words are formed by moving between adjacent circles along the connecting lines, either horizontally, vertically, or diagonally in any direction.

Begin by crossing out the letters already in place, together with the one letter that doesn't appear in any of the words.

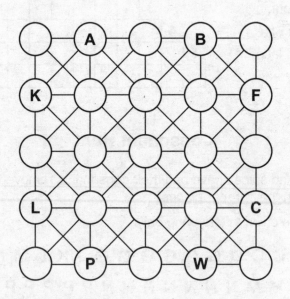

A B C D E F G H I J K L M

N O P Q R S T U V W X Y Z

CROQUET	JAM	RIB
CRUMB	MAKE	SNOWY
DIME	MAXIMUM	SWORD
FIRM	PHLEGM	VIRUS
FROWN	POET	WORM

The Bottom Line

Can you fill each square in the bottom line with the correct letter, to make a five-letter word?

Every square in the solution contains only one letter from each of the numbered lines above, although two or more squares in the solution may contain the same letter.

At the end of every line is a score, which shows:

a   the number of letters placed in the correct finishing position on the bottom line; and

b   the number of letters that appear on the bottom line, but in a different position.

						Correctly Placed	Incorrectly Placed
1	L	A	D	Y	Y	1	2
2	P	O	L	P	O	1	1
3	U	O	U	Y	O	1	1
4	R	A	O	A	L	2	1
5	R	U	B	E	L	1	0
6	E	D	O	D	E	0	1
						5	0

Solutions

1

Here is one possible solution:
SNOW - slow - slot - slat - seat - meat - MELT

2

EMBROIDER

3

DUNE
Neither M, O, S, or T is in the solution (line 1).
Comparing lines 2 and 3, A is not in the
solution, so both N and U are incorrectly
placed (4), and L is not in the solution (2).
In line 3, E is correctly placed. The U isn't
in 3rd (2) or 1st position (4), so 2nd. D is in
the solution (5), so it's 1st. Thus N is in 3rd
position.

4

AFTERSHOCK

5

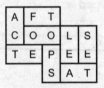

6

7

A	N	E	E	M	A	H	O	K
S	I	G	N	A	T	U	R	E
S	B	O	D	P	E	M	B	Y

8

1 Gallon, 2 Bridle, 3 Amazon, 4 Brandy,
5 Hoarse, 6 Modern.
Creature: LIZARD

9

P	A	P	A	W
S	L	A	V	E
A	G	R	E	E
L	A	I	R	D
M	E	S	S	Y

10

		☆		☆			☆		☆
D	U	M	P	A	P	E	X	F	I	L	M
A	L	G	A	B	E	N	D	I	N	T	O
B	O	U	T	A	N	E	W	I	C	O	N
O	A	T	H	C	I	T	Y	G	U	R	U
P	U	F	F	S	C	U	D	A	L	U	M
T	A	X	I	D	I	V	A	A	P	S	E
C	Y	A	N	C	L	A	W	B	A	R	N
V	I	E	D	F	L	O	P	A	B	U	T
W	A	K	E	M	I	N	X	F	L	E	A
H	E	I	R	O	N	Y	X	Z	E	A	L

11

BASIL
A appears at least once in the solution (line 2)
but not in 1st, 4th or 5th position. Nor is A in
3rd position (line 3), thus (by elimination) A
appears only once, in 2nd position. B and S
are also in the solution (2), thus E is not used
(3). B is in 1st position (1). S is in 3rd position
(5), thus T and D are not used. L is in the
solution (4) in 5th position. I is correctly placed
in 4th position (1).

12

1 Guarded, 2 Argued, 3 Urged, 4 Rude,
5 Cured, 6 Reduce, 7 Secured.

13

The five-letter word is: LOFTY

14

ABLAZE, DILATE, ECLAIR, GALAXY,
PALACE, SALARY

Solutions

15

C	A	P	E	R
A	G	I	L	E
P	I	O	U	S
E	L	U	D	E
R	E	S	E	T

16

A	K	P	S	T
V	U	U	A	A
O	M	M	T	N
C	Q	P	S	G
A	U	K	U	E
D	A	I	M	L
O	T	N	A	O

17

1 Marrow, 2 Strife, 3 Afford, 4 Cradle,
5 Dancer, 6 Future.
Answer: CARROT

18

1 Welcome, 2 Albumen, 3 Lobster, 4 Timothy,
5 Eclipse, 6 Recruit, 7 Sabbath, 8 Confess,
9 Olympus, 10 Tornado, 11 Twinkle.
Walter Scott: *The Bride of Lammermoor*

19

TORN

Comparing lines 1 and 3, S is not in the
solution. If B is in the solution it is in 3rd
position (line 4) and 4th position (line 3), so O
is 2nd position (3). But then D, E, and N aren't
in the solution (4), so T would be in 1st position
(5), and line 1 won't work. So B is not in the
solution. Thus O and R are in 2nd and 3rd
positions (3). E is not in the solution (4). Either
A or N is in the solution (2), so G is not (1). If
A is in the solution, it is in 1st position (2). But
then N is not in the solution (1), so D is in 1st
position (4), which isn't possible if A is 1st. So
A is not in the solution. N is in 4th position (4).
Thus D isn't in the solution (4), so T (5) is in 1st
position.

20

BRIGADIER, CONQUEROR, WATERSHED,
UNETHICAL, FOREIGNER, ORIGINATE,
PROPHETIC, STRANGEST.
The phrase is: INTERIOR DESIGNER

21

1 Capricorn, 2 Labyrinth, 3 Duplicate,
4 Reykjavik, 5 Sanctuary, 6 Greenland,
7 Kampuchea, 8 Orchestra, 9 Jellyfish.

22

Q	U	A	I	N	T		M		T	
U	F			A	P	A	T	H	Y	
A	A			K		R		O		
V	I	R	T	U	E		Z	E	R	O
E		E		N		I		A		
R	A	D	A	R		E	P	O	X	Y
	N	M		E		A			I	
V	I	E	W		J	U	N	G	L	E
	M	O			E		R		L	
F	A	B	R	I	C		I		D	
	L	K		T	H	A	N	K	S	

23

O	U	G	H	T
A		R		
F	L	I	C	K
		M		E
E	V	E	R	Y

24

U	G	L	I	E	S	T
S	P	E	C	I	A	L
M	U	S	I	C	A	L
C	A	P	T	U	R	E
C	L	I	M	A	T	E
A	L	L	E	R	G	Y
E	M	B	R	A	C	E

Solutions

25

E	L	A	P	S	E
B	A	B	O	O	N
Q	U	A	R	T	Z
K	N	O	T	T	Y
S	C	R	E	A	M
C	H	A	R	G	E

26

1 Nod, 2 Below, 3 Compare, 4 Carthorse,
5 Centrifugal, 6 Chrysanthemum.
The word is: DOLPHIN

27

1 Harmonica, 2 Tambourine, 3 Piano,
4 Saxophone, 5 Concertina, 6 Ukulele,
7 Violin, 8 Clarinet, 9 Bassoon, 10 Guitar,
11 Mandolin, 12 Piccolo.

28

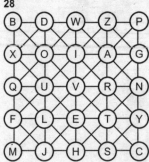

29

TUSK
Comparing lines 2 and 3, L is not in the
solution. Comparing lines 2 and 5, E is not in
the solution, so S is (line 2). Comparing lines 3
and 5, if I is in the solution, it is in both 2nd and
3rd positions, so S would be in 1st position (2),
and K would not be in the solution (3). But then
line 5 can't work. So I is not in the solution.
Thus in line 5, U is in 2nd position and K is
in 4th position in the solution. A isn't in the
solution (3). Either T or N is in the solution (1)
so there's no G (4). S is in 3rd position (4) so T
is in 1st position (1).

30

Here is one possible solution:
GOAT - boat - beat - peat - peas - pegs - PIGS

31

DISBELIEF

32

UPHOLSTERY

33

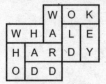

34

35

L	C	D	O	U	S	D	I	S
Y	A	R	D	S	T	I	C	K
E	M	Y	E	E	Y	M	Y	Y

36

1 Mascot, 2 Adhere, 3 Appear, 4 Cornet,
5 Zagreb, 6 Anyhow.
Fruit: CHERRY

37

M	A	G	M	A
A	R	R	A	S
D	E	A	N	S
A	N	I	S	E
M	A	N	E	S

Solutions

38

			☆		☆				☆		☆
W	A	R	M	A	L	S	O	A	B	E	T
E	C	H	O	B	U	S	H	H	A	I	R
W	R	E	N	A	M	O	K	I	N	C	A
D	I	V	A	O	B	O	E	S	K	I	M
V	E	E	R	B	E	L	T	W	R	A	P
L	A	I	C	B	R	E	W	J	U	D	O
W	I	S	H	A	J	A	R	O	P	A	L
Y	E	T	I	P	A	R	K	E	T	U	I
P	I	G	S	A	C	N	E	S	C	A	N
J	U	S	T	S	K	U	A	T	Y	P	E

39

HOWL

If B is in 1st position (line 2), then it is also in 3rd (line 4) and E and L aren't in the solution. But then line 5 won't work. So B is not in the solution (2 and 4), thus O is in the solution (2). If D is used, then it's in 1st position (4) and E and L are not used. But then both I and W are in the solution (5), and I would also be in 1st position, which isn't possible. So D is not in the solution. If E is in the solution, then L is not (4), thus both C and H are in the solution (3), which isn't possible (1). So E is not in the solution. L is in 4th position (4). I and S are not in the solution (1), so W is in 3rd position (5). O is in 2nd position (2). The letter in 1st position isn't C (3), so H.

40

1 Thermal, 2 *Hamlet*, 3 Metal, 4 Team, 5 Mated, 6 Tandem, 7 Untamed.

41

The five-letter word is: TRAWL

42

ASTUTE, FUTURE, MUTUAL, OBTUSE, RETURN, ROTUND

43

F	L	A	M	E
L	O	S	E	R
A	S	I	D	E
M	E	D	I	C
E	R	E	C	T

44

M	E	B	N	F
O	C	E	A	I
R	U	L	M	N
O	A	G	I	L
C	D	I	B	A
C	O	U	I	N
O	R	M	A	D

45

1 Sermon, 2 Doctor, 3 Hammer, 4 Mutiny, 5 Writer, 6 Police.
Answer: EMPIRE

46

1 Sardine, 2 Tadpole, 3 Ecstasy, 4 Pacific, 5 Hammock, 6 Educate, 7 Namibia, 8 Kitchen, 9 Illegal, 10 Neptune, 11 Garland.
Stephen King: *The Eyes of the Dragon*

47

MOAT

If T is not in the solution, then (lines 3 and 4) M, D, O, A, and E are all in the solution (which isn't possible). So T is in the solution and (1) S and Y are not. O is in the solution (5). If D is in the solution (3), then M isn't, and (2) one of either U or R is in the solution. But then line 4 doesn't work. So D isn't in the solution. M is in the solution (3) and (2) U and R are not. T isn't in 2nd position (1), so M is in 1st position (2). O isn't in 3rd or 4th position (5), so 2nd. T isn't in 3rd position (3), so 4th. Thus the letter correctly placed in line 4 is A, in 3rd position.

48

PANTOMIME, HEADCOUNT, ENTRANCED, UNINSURED, PROXIMITY, HUNDREDTH, GUARANTOR, DALMATIAN.
The phrase is: NATIONAL MONUMENT

49

1 Discharge, 2 Butterfly, 3 Acquiesce, 4 Earthworm, 5 Eavesdrop, 6 Beautiful, 7 Nefertiti, 8 Bookshelf, 9 Astronomy.

Solutions

50

C	A	R	D		B		F		F
A		A		C	A	R	A	V	A	N
T	A	G	S		G		R		N
A		S	Q	U	E	A	M	I	S	H
C			U		L		S		O
O	C	E	A	N		O	T	T	E	R
M			W		J		E		S
B	A	C	K	P	E	D	A	L		E
	N		I		W		D	A	U	B
M	E	A	N	D	E	R		Z		O
	W		G		L		L	Y	N	X

51

		B		S
S	C	A	M	P
T		K		R
E	N	E	M	Y
W		R		

52

S	E	G	M	E	N	T
T	H	Y	R	O	I	D
A	N	A	R	C	H	Y
C	O	C	K	P	I	T
M	I	L	L	I	O	N
M	E	T	H	A	N	E
D	U	C	K	I	N	G

53

D	E	C	A	M	P
S	Q	U	E	A	L
J	U	G	G	L	E
P	I	G	E	O	N
I	N	F	A	N	T
K	E	E	N	L	Y

54

1 Urn, 2 Float, 3 Another, 4 Athletics,
5 Recruitment, 6 Environmental.
The word is: PROTEIN

55

1 Diamond, 2 Sapphire, 3 Emerald, 4 Peridot,
5 Amethyst, 6 Topaz, 7 Ruby, 8 Beryl,
9 Tourmaline, 10 Aquamarine, 11 Opal,
12 Turquoise.

56

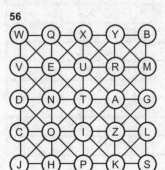

57

VEIL

If O is in the solution, then only one of C, L or I is in the solution (line 3), which isn't possible (line 1). So O is not in the solution. Two of either C, L or I are in the solution (3), so E is also in the solution (1). It isn't in 4th (1), 3rd (2) or 1st position (4), so 2nd. Either W or V is in the solution (5), so C isn't (4). L and I are in the solution (1). L isn't in 1st (1) or 3rd position (3), so 4th. W isn't in 3rd (4) or 1st position (5), so W is not in the solution. Thus V is in 1st position (5). I is in 3rd position (3).

58

Here is one possible solution:
SINK - sank - sand - said - skid - skim – SWIM

59

LIMELIGHT

60

JOURNALISM

61

A	P	T		
R	E	A	C	T
C	A	N	O	E
		S	P	A

Solutions

62

A	L	I	B	I		G			
N		N		N		E	M	U	
T	E	N	S	I	O	N		N	
E				T		I	L	L	
A		S	E	I	Z	E		O	
T	O	O		A				O	
E		B	I	L	I	O	U	S	
R	U	E		L		V		E	
		R		Y	E	A	R	N	

63

I	J	A	S	H	A	H	A	R
M	A	C	H	I	N	E	R	Y
P	B	E	Y	P	D	M	C	E

64

1 Exodus, 2 Change, 3 Anchor, 4 Beluga,
5 Gemini, 6 Flawed.
Flower: DAHLIA

65

C	A	P	R	I
O	R	L	O	N
B	E	A	U	S
R	A	N	G	E
A	S	S	E	T

66

C	H	E	F	I	B	E	X	K	N	O	B
H	E	R	O	P	A	C	K	V	I	S	A
B	O	A	R	S	C	A	M	A	G	A	R
F	A	R	M	S	K	E	W	C	H	U	B
M	A	G	I	A	G	O	G	S	T	O	A
C	L	O	D	B	R	E	W	E	M	I	R
C	O	L	A	J	O	K	E	T	A	X	I
G	R	A	B	T	U	R	F	U	R	E	A
C	O	W	L	G	N	A	W	V	E	I	N
W	I	F	E	I	D	E	A	A	S	K	S

67

PASS

Either O or P is in the solution (line 5), so E
and G aren't (line 2). At most, only one of A or
L is in the solution (1), so S is in the solution (4)
and V isn't (3). Either A or L is in the solution
(4), so O isn't (1). P is in the solution (2). P isn't
in 2nd (2), 3rd or 4th position (5), so 1st. The
letter in 2nd position isn't P (2), S (3) or L (4),
so (by elimination) A, and there is no L (1). The
letter in 3rd position isn't A (1) or P (5), so S.
The letter in 4th position isn't A (4) or P (5), so
S.

68

1 Bearing, 2 Regain, 3 Anger, 4, Gear,
5 Agree, 6 Regale, 7 General.

69

The five-letter word is: AZURE

70

ADVENT, CAVEAT, COVERS, DIVERT,
GOVERN, REVEAL

71

T	R	A	S	H
R	O	D	E	O
A	D	D	E	R
S	E	E	D	S
H	O	R	S	E

72

A	C	I	M	R

N	O	C	A	E

T	R	E	J	U

I	S	L	O	N

G	I	A	R	I

U	C	N	C	O

A	A	D	A	N

73

1 Karate, 2 Sprang, 3 Acacia, 4 Lethal,
5 Poetry, 6 Clinch.
Answer: PICKLE

74

1 Dahomey, 2 Absence, 3 Niagara, 4 Iceland,
5 Emerald, 6 Lanolin, 7 Decibel, 8 Exhaled,
9 Finally, 10 Octagon, 11 Entwine.
Daniel Defoe: *Robinson Crusoe*

Solutions

75

WARM

There is at most one of D or A in the solution (line 3), so there's also at least one M (line 5). There is no M in 3rd (2) 1st or 2nd position (5), so M is in 4th position. There is no O, E or D (2), so A is in the solution (5), but not in 3rd position, nor 1st (3), so 2nd. T is not in the solution (3). R is in the solution (1) in 3rd position. W (4) is in 1st position.

76

MICROCOSM, BEHEMOTHS, TREADMILL, HOMEOPATH, REINFORCE, DECIDUOUS, DRAGONFLY, CELANDINE.
The phrase is: CHEMICAL COMPOUND

77

1 Satellite, 2 Uncertain, 3 Nostalgia, 4 Beethoven, 5 Explosion, 6 Ambiguous, 7 Mayflower, 8 Snowflake, 9 Bodyguard.

78

K	N	E	A	D		S		A		C
	A			U	N	L	U	C	K	Y
Q	U	A	L	M		O		H		A
	T		B	E	T	W	E	E	N	
J	I	G	S		X		I		F	
	C		C	H	I	P	S		F	
	A		U		L		P	O	U	T
B	L	A	D	D	E	R			S	
R		W		R		U	N	Z	I	P
A	R	R	E	A	R	S			V	
N		Y		G		T	H	R	E	W

79

S		M		E
Q	U	I	L	T
U		L		H
A	N	K	L	E
D		Y		R

80

R	I	C	H	A	R	D
M	A	U	R	I	C	E
R	O	Y	S	T	O	N
C	L	E	M	E	N	T
G	R	E	G	O	R	Y
A	N	T	H	O	N	Y
W	I	L	F	R	E	D

81

Q	U	E	B	E	C
S	P	O	O	K	Y
T	H	R	O	N	G
M	O	L	T	E	N
F	L	E	E	C	E
A	D	V	E	N	T

82

2 Pit, 3 Laces, 4 Blocked, 5 Gunpowder, 6 Consolidate, 7 Accommodation.
The word is: PICCOLO

83

1 Madrid, 2 Vienna, 3 Oslo, 4 Bratislava, 5 Copenhagen, 6 Paris, 7 Lisbon, 8 Stockholm, 9 Zagreb, 10 Warsaw, 11 London, 12 Amsterdam.

84

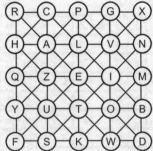

85

OPEN

L isn't in 3rd (line 1), 1st (line 2), 2nd (3) or 4th position (4), so there is no L. If E isn't in the solution, there is H and O (1) and A and P (2), so line 3 can't work. Thus E is in, but not in 4th (1), 2nd (2) or 1st (3), so 3rd position. There is only one of A or P (2), so (4) N is in the solution. N isn't in 2nd (4) or 1st (5), so 4th

Solutions

position. I is not in the solution (3). H isn't in 1st (1) or 2nd (5), so there is no H; thus (1) O is in 1st position. There is no A (5), so (2) the letter in 2nd position is P.

86

Here is one possible solution:
CITY - pity - pits - pots - tots - tows - TOWN

87

MUTILATES and STIMULATE

88

ECONOMICAL

89

90

91

A	S	I	A	Z	E	V	A	E
P	A	R	S	I	M	O	N	Y
T	W	K	K	P	U	W	Y	E

92

1 Eiffel, 2 Breath, 3 Bronze, 4 Monaco,
5 Asleep, 6 Bullet.
Herb: FENNEL

93

P	A	S	T	A
A	G	A	R	S
R	O	L	E	S
K	R	O	N	A
S	A	N	D	Y

94

L	I	M	P	F	R	E	T	H	A	R	P
L	A	V	A	D	E	N	Y	A	L	S	O
E	V	I	L	A	G	O	G	P	L	U	S
R	A	N	I	B	U	R	N	J	I	L	T
D	A	M	P	F	L	U	X	A	T	O	M
K	I	N	D	B	A	R	B	V	E	T	O
J	E	E	R	S	T	U	B	G	R	I	D
H	E	R	O	G	I	F	T	C	A	F	E
O	V	U	M	B	O	O	K	S	T	A	R
D	U	K	E	K	N	E	W	K	E	E	N

95

OBOE
There is one letter from line 1 and two from line 2; and lines 1 and 2 contain all the letters, so there are only three letters in the solution, thus one is duplicated. S isn't in 4th position (line 2), 1st or 2nd (line 3) or 3rd (4), so there is no S. Thus O and E are both in the solution (3), so there is no A, R or Y (1). B is in the solution (4), so L is not in the solution (2). B isn't in 3rd (2), 1st or 4th position (4), so 2nd. E isn't in 3rd (3) or 1st (5), so 4th position. There are thus two Os, in 1st and 3rd position.

96

1 Descent, 2 Nested, 3 Dense, 4 Send,
5 Needs, 6 Sensed, 7 Endless.

97

The five-letter word is: CRYPT

98

BESTOW, BISTRO, CUSTOM, INSTEP,
PASTEL, RUSTLE

99

V	E	R	S	E
E	X	A	C	T
R	A	J	A	H
S	C	A	R	E
E	T	H	E	R

Solutions

100

C	G	M	P	R
A	I	A	A	A
R	R	C	N	C
I	A	A	T	C
B	F	Q	H	O
O	F	U	E	O
U	E	E	R	N

101

1 Arabic, 2 Beyond, 3 Fabric, 4 Ritual,
5 Sudden, 6 Safari.
Answer: FRIDAY

102

1 Hepburn, 2 Ecuador, 3 Nursery, 4 Recluse,
5 Yashmak, 6 Majorca, 7 Ignored, 8 Luggage,
9 Leopard, 10 Elastic, 11 Relaxed.
Henry Miller: *Tropic of Capricorn*

103

SITE
M isn't in 1st position (line 1), 4th (line 3), 2nd
(4) or 3rd (5), so there is no M. U isn't in 2nd
position (1), 1st (3), 3rd (4) or 4th (5), so there
is no U. Thus there are S and T (1), as well
as E and I (3) in the solution, so not L or O
(2). I isn't in 4th (2), 3rd (3) or 1st (4), so 2nd
position. T isn't in 4th (1) or 1st (5), so 3rd.
E isn't in 1st position (2), so 4th. S is in 1st
position.

104

PARACHUTE, THESAURUS, GOLDSMITH,
CLASSICAL, EXTRADITE, HAIRPIECE,
LIVESTOCK, CLERGYMAN.
The phrase is: RELATIVE HUMIDITY

105

1 Frequency, 2 Overwhelm, 3 Legendary,
4 Liberated, 5 Opportune, 6 Warehouse,
7 Ignorance, 8 Nectarine, 9 Gunpowder.

106

107

108

P	I	L	G	R	I	M
A	R	A	B	I	A	N
E	T	E	R	N	A	L
B	A	S	S	O	O	N
S	T	I	M	U	L	I
C	O	S	T	U	M	E
N	O	W	H	E	R	E

109

T	A	R	I	F	F
C	R	E	N	E	L
F	R	I	D	A	Y
G	E	M	I	N	I
I	S	O	G	O	N
S	T	R	O	N	G

110

1 Not, 2 Timed, 3 Adopted, 4 Amusement,
5 Beneficiary, 6 Advertisement.
The word is: POMPEII

111

1 Exodus, 2 Psalms, 3 Mark, 4 Numbers,
5 Luke, 6 Jonah, 7 Job, 8 Genesis, 9 Ezra,
10 Hebrews, 11 Matthew, 12 Daniel.

Solutions

112

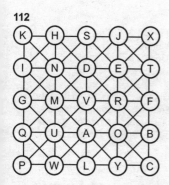

113

TOUR

If both I and T are in the solution, then neither O nor M is (line 1), nor U or E (line 3), so S and R are both in the solution (2). S isn't 3rd (4), so R would be 4th (2), I 1st (5) and S 2nd (4). But then line 3 doesn't work. O and M aren't both in the solution (4). So either I or T is in, as is either O or M (1), thus not E or S (4). So U and R are in the solution (2). There is no M or I in the solution (5), so both O and T are in (1). The letter in 4th position isn't T (1) or O (4). If U is 4th, then line 2 doesn't work - so R is 4th. U is 3rd (5). O isn't 1st (1), so 2nd. T is 1st.

114

Here is one possible solution:
COAL - coat - moat - most - mist - mint - MINE

115

GYROSCOPE

116

TRAMPOLINE

117

T	U	G		
E	R	O	D	E
A	N	N	U	L
		G	E	M

118

A	D	R	O	I	T		T	
L		A			A	F	A	R
P	O	D		C	O	A	X	
A		I		H		B	I	T
C		A	D	I	E	U		U
A	C	T		E		L		R
	H	O	O	F		O	W	E
G	U	R	U			U		E
	M		R	E	A	S	O	N

119

T	H	T	S	O	K	G	A	S
W	O	R	K	B	E	N	C	H
O	W	Y	I	I	G	U	T	E

120

1 Carpet, 2 Frothy, 3 Almost, 4 Budget,
5 Merlin, 6 Beetle.
Breed of dog: POODLE

121

C	R	E	S	S
L	A	M	I	A
A	D	O	R	N
M	A	T	E	D
P	R	E	S	S

122

G	L	I	B	A	F	A	R	J	A	M	B
C	O	I	L	J	A	Z	Z	A	S	I	A
I	O	T	A	F	R	O	G	S	T	I	R
E	P	I	C	E	S	P	Y	T	R	U	E
D	O	C	K	F	I	Z	Z	B	O	T	H
K	I	S	S	U	G	L	Y	K	N	E	E
F	I	R	M	T	H	A	W	Y	O	G	A
K	I	W	I	S	T	Y	E	A	M	I	D
J	I	L	T	F	E	U	D	W	E	R	E
H	U	S	H	E	D	G	Y	B	R	E	D

Solutions

123

MONK

E isn't in 4th position (line 1), 2nd (line 2), 1st (4) or 3rd (5) position, so there is no E. N isn't in 1st (1), 4th (4) or 2nd (5) position - and I isn't in 2nd (1), 4th (2) or 1st (3) position, so there is only one of either N or I (1), in 3rd position. Thus K is in the solution (1). If A is in the solution, then M and I are not (3). But then line 2 doesn't work. So A is not in the solution. At most one of M or I is in the solution (3), thus O is in the solution (2). Either S or N is also in the solution (5), so M is in the solution (4) and I is not (2). N is in the solution (1), so S is not (4). N isn't in 1st (1), 4th (4) or 2nd position (5), so 3rd. O isn't in 1st (2) or 4th (5), so 2nd position. M isn't in 4th position (3), so 1st. K is in 4th position.

124

1 Algebra, 2 Arable, 3 Blare, 4 Real, 5 Clear, 6 Cradle, 7 Crawled.

125

The five-letter word is: FIRST

126

BECAME, ESCAPE, FACADE, LOCALE, RECALL, VACATE

127

C	H	A	S	M
H	A	S	T	E
A	S	H	E	N
S	T	E	E	D
M	E	N	D	S

128

B	C	D	J	S
E	O	E	A	M
R	P	L	N	E
L	L	I	A	T
I	A	B	C	A
O	N	E	E	N
Z	D	S	K	A

129

1 Sprawl, 2 Temper, 3 Turbot, 4 Burrow, 5 Stanza, 6 Walnut.
Answer: SATURN

130

1 Regular, 2 Ukulele, 3 Thirsty, 4 Honesty, 5 Rossini, 6 Entered, 7 Nonagon, 8 Diamond, 9 Elegant, 10 Lettuce, 11 Lincoln.
Ruth Rendell: *The Face of Trespass*

131

HERB

If C is in the solution, then only one of R, S or B is in (line 4). Thus (line 2) U is in, as is only one of A, H or E (3), so (5) S is in. But of C, U and S, none is in 3rd position (1, 2 and 3) or 2nd position (2, 4 and 5), so these three letters would be in 1st and/or 4th position, which isn't possible. Thus there is no C in the solution. There are two of either R, B and S in the solution (4), so no U (2). There are two of either E, H and A (3), so no S (5). R and B are in the solution (2). R isn't in 2nd (1), 4th (2) or 1st position (4), so 3rd. Either A or H is in the solution (1), so E is also in the solution (3). E isn't in 1st (3) or 4th position (5), so 2nd. B isn't in 1st position (2), so 4th. The letter in 1st position isn't A (1), so H.

132

EXTROVERT, FREQUENCY, CORPULENT, DUMBFOUND, BRIEFCASE, CONSCIOUS, FLAUNTING, KILOBYTES.
The phrase is: TERMINAL VELOCITY

133

1 Nightclub, 2 Firepower, 3 Arabesque, 4 Venezuela, 5 Badminton, 6 Adjective, 7 Mousetrap, 8 Corkscrew, 9 Abyssinia.

134

Solutions

135

P	E	D	A	L
■	Q	■	S	■
B	U	M	P	Y
■	I	■	E	■
S	P	E	N	D

136

A	B	I	G	A	I	L
A	N	N	A	B	E	L
L	E	T	I	T	I	A
M	A	D	O	N	N	A
Y	O	L	A	N	D	E
N	A	T	A	L	I	E
J	E	S	S	I	C	A

137

S	P	R	A	N	G
C	A	R	T	E	L
Q	U	A	R	T	O
A	N	T	I	C	S
O	C	C	U	R	S
W	H	I	M	S	Y

138

1 Dew, 2 Melon, 3 Brigade, 4 Abominate,
5 Agriculture, 6 Complimentary.
The word is: BELGIUM

139

1 Hadrian, 2 Diocletian, 3 Augustus,
4 Caligula, 5 Tiberius, 6 Constantine, 7 Trajan,
8 Postumus, 9 Nero, 10 Galba, 11 Tacitus,
12 Claudius.

140

141

IDEA
There are two of A, U, L and D (line 1) and
two of S, I, O and E (line 4), so there are four
different letters in the solution. If O is in the
solution, there is no S, A or U (2), so L and
D are both in (1), as is I (3) - but then line 5
doesn't work. Thus there is no O. If S is in the
solution, then A and U aren't (2), so L and D
are in the solution (1), as is I (5) - but then line
3 doesn't work. Thus there is no S. I and E are
both in the solution (4). If L is in the solution,
then A isn't (5), so U is in (2), thus not D (1).
But then U isn't in 4th position (2), so I is in
1st (3), L in 2nd (5) and U in 3rd position (2).
But then E would be in 4th position, which
isn't possible (4). So there is no L. A is in the
solution (5), so U isn't (2). D is in the solution
(1). The letter in 4th position isn't D (1) or E (4).
If I is in 4th position, then line 5 doesn't work,
so A is in 4th position. I isn't in 2nd (4) or 3rd
(5), so 1st position. D isn't in 3rd (3), so 2nd
position. E is in 3rd position.

142

Here is one possible solution:
NEWT - neat - beat - bent - bend - bond - POND

143

BRIEFCASE

144

INSPECTION

145

146

E	R	■	Q	■	F	■	O
A	G	O	■	U	N	I	O	N
S	■	T	E	A	■	L	■	T
E	R	A	■	L	I	M	B	O
■	I	■	I	■	■	O	■
S	P	O	O	F	■	W	O	E
E	■	P	■	I	C	E	■	P
A	Z	U	R	E	■	A	P	E
M	■	S	■	D	■	K	■	E

Solutions

147

C	O	I	P	A	A	W	S	S
O	W	N	E	R	S	H	I	P
G	L	N	W	M	H	Y	X	A

148

1 Mayfly, 2 Barrel, 3 Salami, 4 Cancel,
5 Muscat, 6 Speaks.
Country: FRANCE

149

P	A	C	T	S
L	I	L	A	C
A	R	O	M	A
N	E	V	E	R
T	R	E	S	S

150

G	A	R	B	B	R	A	Y	F	I	R	M
S	A	R	I	B	E	S	T	U	N	D	O
D	A	W	N	S	P	R	Y	M	A	L	T
D	A	D	O	B	U	R	Y	S	U	C	H
Z	I	N	C	I	B	E	X	O	G	R	E
E	C	R	U	F	L	O	W	P	U	R	R
B	A	W	L	F	I	L	M	O	R	A	L
F	L	E	A	S	C	U	T	P	A	P	A
E	W	E	R	T	A	S	K	S	T	U	N
A	L	A	S	S	N	O	W	L	E	W	D

151

PUMP

If G is in the solution, there is no E, R or U
(line 2), so only one of M or B (line 3). But then
P is in (5) and not M or O (4). But then line 1
doesn't work. So there is no G. There are two
of M, U and B (3), so O is not in the solution
(1). Thus M and P are in the solution (4) and B
and E are not (5). U is in the solution (1), so R
is not (2). Thus only the letters U, M, P are in
the solution. The letter in 1st position isn't U (1)
or M (4), so P. The letter correctly place in 2nd
position (3) is U. The letter in 4th position isn't
U (2) or M (5), so P. M is in 3rd position.

152

1 Enticed, 2 Deceit, 3 Edict, 4 Tied, 5 Tepid,
6 Depict, 7 Predict.

153

The five-letter word is: PARTY

154

ADMIRE, COMING, DEMISE, ENMITY,
FAMINE, SIMILE

155

C	A	R	G	O
A	C	O	R	N
R	O	B	E	S
G	R	E	B	E
O	N	S	E	T

156

A	B	C	R	S

R	U	A	U	W

A	R	T	S	A

M	M	A	S	H

A	E	L	I	I

I	S	A	A	L

C	E	N	N	I

157

1 Object, 2 Honest, 3 Trench, 4 Worker,
5 Squire, 6 Cinder.
Answer: BOOTED

158

1 Scarlet, 2 Younger, 3 Lapland, 4 Vertigo,
5 Iceberg, 6 Agitate, 7 Patrick, 8 Lebanon,
9 Alabama, 10 Tequila, 11 Hendrix.
Sylvia Plath: *Crossing the Water*

159

GIFT

If both K and T are in the solution (line 1), then
there's no N or I, no G or C (line 3) and no O
or F (4), so line 5 doesn't work. If neither K nor
T is in the solution (1), then the solution has N
and I, as well as G and C (3) and line 4 doesn't
work. Thus we've one of K or T, as well as
one of N or I (1). We've also one of G or C (3)
and one of F or O (4), so 4 different letters. In
line 4, if F is correctly placed in 1st position,
then O is not in the solution (above), and I
is in 4th position (2) - but then line 1 doesn't

Solutions

work. In line 4, if K is correctly placed in 2nd position, then T is not in the solution (above), I is in 3rd position (1) and C is in 1st position (2) - and line 3 doesn't work. In line 4, if O is correctly placed in 3rd position, then F is not in the solution (above) and we've either C correctly placed in 1st or I correctly placed in 4th position (2). If C is in 1st position, then T is in 2nd (3) and line 1 doesn't work. If I is in 4th position, then N is not in the solution (above), so G is in 2nd position (5) and line 3 doesn't work. So in line 4, the correctly placed letter is T, and (above) K is not in the solution. G is correctly placed (3) in 1st position, so C is not in the solution (above). F is in 3rd position (5), so O is not in the solution (above). The letter in 2nd position isn't N (1), so I.

160

IMPRECISE, DEERHOUND, SCREAMING, DISAPPEAR, PROTRUDED, HANDSTAND, EVANGELIC, VELODROME.
The phrase is: PERSONAL COMPUTER

161

1 Remainder, 2 Absorbent, 3 Geography, 4 Parchment, 5 Jerusalem, 6 Caribbean, 7 Eliminate, 8 Afterward, 9 Lithuania.

162

F	A	L	S	E		G	R	O	W	L
A		E		X		U		B		A
T	R	A	M	P		R		J	A	W
E		P		A	Z	U	R	E		Y
				N				C		E
S	Q	U	I	D		T	U	T	O	R
O		N				H				
N		H	A	L	V	E		B		V
A	D	O		A		S	T	O	V	E
T		O		C		I		N		N
A	N	K	L	E		S	W	E	E	T

163

R	E	C	A	P
E		O		L
T	H	Y	M	E
I		P		A
E	X	U	L	T

164

S	C	A	L	L	O	P
C	U	L	T	U	R	E
I	M	P	R	E	S	S
C	H	A	P	T	E	R
P	L	A	T	O	O	N
B	R	A	V	E	R	Y
E	X	H	A	U	S	T

165

J	O	Y	F	U	L
A	B	L	A	Z	E
S	T	A	M	E	N
V	A	R	I	E	D
T	I	S	S	U	E
A	N	C	H	O	R

166

1 Got, 2 Maple, 3 Abreast, 4 Headfirst, 5 Articulated, 6 Uncomplicated.
The word is: HOPEFUL

167

1 Botticelli, 2 Picasso, 3 Warhol, 4 Constable, 5 Tintoretto, 6 Brueghel, 7 Michelangelo, 8 Caravaggio, 9 Turner, 10 Rembrandt, 11 Canaletto, 12 Gainsborough.

168

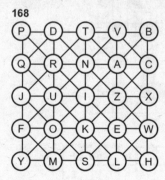

169

TROT
There is only one of either U, T, B or E (line 1) and only two of either R, L, O, I (line 3), so there is a duplicate letter. If E is in the solution, then it's in 4th position (1) and there's no U, T or B, so two different letters from I, R or O (2). But then there's no L (3), so line 4 doesn't work. So there is no E. If B is in the solution,

Solutions

then there's no O or I (5), so R and L (3) are in the solution, and T is not (4), so U is correctly placed in 2nd position (1). But then the letter in 1st position isn't B (2), R (3) or L (4), so this isn't possible. Thus there's no B, so there is one of O or I (5), plus R (2), so no L (3). Thus T is in the solution (4), in 1st position (1). U isn't in the solution (1). R isn't in 3rd (2) or 4th (4), so 2nd position. The letter in 3rd position isn't I (3) or T (4), so O. I is not in the solution (3). The letter in 4th position isn't O (2) or R (4), so T.

170
Here is one possible solution:
WASH - lash - last - lost - loot - root - ROOM

171
GENEALOGY

172
KINGFISHER

173

174

175

F	I	I	G	P	H	E	P	F
I	N	C	U	R	A	B	L	E
T	K	E	M	Y	Y	B	Y	W

176
1 Flower, 2 Abacus, 3 Dragon, 4 Runway, 5 Rarest, 6 Carrot.
Composer: WAGNER

177

A	L	P	H	A
S	O	L	O	S
T	I	E	R	S
E	R	A	S	E
R	E	S	E	T

178

☆		☆			☆		☆
L	A	M	A	O	B	E	Y	F	A	K	E
C	O	R	N	B	R	A	Y	A	P	E	X
A	B	E	T	B	A	R	K	E	P	I	C
T	U	N	A	H	I	N	T	U	R	D	U
F	R	O	G	K	N	E	W	B	E	L	L
U	N	D	O	S	P	R	Y	S	N	A	P
C	Y	A	N	B	O	O	K	S	T	O	A
Y	E	T	I	S	W	I	M	D	I	R	T
B	O	S	S	P	E	L	T	A	C	N	E
W	H	A	T	T	R	U	E	W	E	L	D

179
STOP
If T and F are both in the solution, there is no S or I (line 1), A or O (line 2), E or P (3). But then lines 4 and 5 won't work. If neither T nor F is in, then both S and I are (1), as well as A and O (2), and line 3 won't work. So one of T or F is in the solution, plus one of I or S (1), one of O or A (2) and one of E or P (3). If T is in the solution and is correctly placed in line 1, then it isn't correctly placed in lines 2 or 3; and we have no F, thus A is in 3rd position (2) and line 3 doesn't work. If F is in the solution and is correctly placed in line 1, we have no T, so O is correct in line 2 and line 3 doesn't work. So the letter correctly placed in line 1 isn't T or F. I isn't in 2nd position (5), so S is in 1st position (1) and there is no I. If F is in the solution, then it's in 4th position (1), so E is in 3rd position (3) and line 5 doesn't work. Thus F isn't in the solution (4), so T is in, but not in 4th position (1). E isn't in 3rd position (5), so P is correctly placed in 4th (3) and there is no E. A isn't in the solution (4). Thus O is in (2), but not in 4th position (P, above), so T is correctly placed in 2nd position (2) and O is in 3rd position.

180
1 Martian, 2 Tirana, 3 Train, 4 Iran, 5 Brain, 6 Riband, 7 Brigand.

Solutions

181
The five-letter word is: VALID

182
ASHORE, BEHOLD, COHORT, ECHOED, SCHOOL, UNHOLY

183

C	A	T	C	H
A	F	I	R	E
T	I	M	E	R
C	R	E	D	O
H	E	R	O	N

184

G	H	I	L	N
E	E	F	E	O
T	Y	I	T	R
B	J	F	I	E
A	U	E	T	P
C	D	L	B	L
K	E	L	E	Y

185
1 Psyche, 2 Matrix, 3 Sacred, 4 Inured,
5 Splash, 6 Tundra.
Answer: EXHALE

186
1 Morocco, 2 Acrobat, 3 Receive, 4 Yucatan,
5 Squeeze, 6 Houdini, 7 Elevate, 8 Lighter,
9 Learned, 10 Explore, 11 Yielded.
Mary Shelley: *The Last Man*

187
DINE
If D and T are both in the solution, there is no I (line 1), E or F (line 2), so line 3 can't work. If neither D nor T is in, A and I are both in (1), as are E and F (2) and line 3 can't work. Thus one of either D or T is in, as is one of either E or F (2), so one of either A or I (1), and one of either O or N (4), making four different letters. Since one of E or F is in the solution, one of I or O is also in (3). If A is in, then I isn't (above), so (3) O is in (3) and N isn't (4); also D and E aren't in the solution (5), so T and F are (above). If A is

in the solution, then it isn't in 4th position (5), so the letter correctly placed in line 4 would be O. A would not be 1st (1) or 4th (5), so 2nd. But then T would not be 4th (1), so 1st, and line 2 doesn't work. So A is not in the solution. Thus I is in the solution (above), as are either E or F. Thus O is not in the solution (3). N is in the solution (4), as are D and E (5). Neither T (1) nor F (2) are in the solution. If E is in 1st position, then line 2 can't work, so D is 1st (2). I is 2nd (3). E isn't in 3rd position (5), so 4th. N is in 3rd position.

188
OBSESSION, ENTRAPPED, PARAMEDIC, RAINWATER, UNCORKING, NOTORIOUS, CULMINATE, SKYLIGHTS.
The phrase is: STRICTLY SPEAKING

189
1 Exclusive, 2 Affluence, 3 Delicious,
4 Carnivore, 5 Roosevelt, 6 Knowledge,
7 Livestock, 8 Vermilion, 9 Negotiate.

190

E	Q	U	I	P		M		B		U
X		N		L	E	A	D	I	N	G
C	O	P	R	A		U		L		L
I		A		N	O	V	E	L	T	Y
T	W	I	N	K	L	E				
E		D		D			R		W	
			R	E	F	R	E	S	H	
C	O	N	J	U	R	E		B		E
H		I		M		A	W	O	K	E
O	M	N	I	B	U	S		R		Z
P		E	A		T	A	N	G	Y	

191

	D	A	W	N
	E		I	
F	L	U	T	E
	A		C	
M	Y	T	H	

Solutions

192

V	A	N	I	L	L	A
P	I	Q	U	A	N	T
L	A	C	T	O	S	E
B	A	T	T	E	R	Y
S	C	H	O	O	L	S
D	E	N	M	A	R	K
R	O	Y	A	L	T	Y

193

S	U	R	F	E	R
E	S	C	A	P	E
H	U	M	B	U	G
G	R	I	L	L	E
D	E	M	E	A	N
C	R	E	D	I	T

194

1 Ale, 2 Globe, 3 Tactile, 4 Ferocious,
5 Grasshopper, 6 Carbohydrates.
The word is: BLOTCHY

195

1 Kentucky, 2 Wisconsin, 3 Oklahoma,
4 Hawaii, 5 California, 6 Texas, 7 Nebraska,
8 Louisiana, 9 Montana, 10 Wyoming,
11 Oregon, 12 Alaska.

196

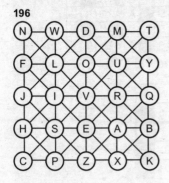

197

SODA

If both D and E are in the solution, then N
and O are not in the solution (line 5), nor is A
(line 1), so line 2 can't work. If both N and O
are in, then D and E aren't (5), nor is A (2), so
line 1 can't work. Thus there is one of D or E
and one of N or O (5), also one of A or I (1) and
one of G or S (4), amounting to four letters.

If I is in, then A isn't, so G is in (2), but not S
(4). In line 4, either G would be 1st or I would
be 3rd. If G is 1st (4), O is correctly placed in
2nd position (2), so I is 4th (4) - but then line
3 doesn't work. If I is 3rd (4), then E is 4th (1)
and G 2nd (4) - but then line 5 doesn't work.
So I is not in the solution. A is in the solution
(above), together with either N or O (2 and
above). Thus G is not in the solution (2), so S
is in the solution (4). If S is 2nd, then the letter
in 4th position is D (3). But then A is correctly
placed in 1st position (1), and line 2 doesn't
work. Thus in line 4, A is in 4th position. D is
in 3rd position (1) and there is no E. S is in 1st
position (3). O is in 2nd position (2).

198

Here is one possible solution:
SOFT - sort - sore - core - care - card - HARD

199

CARTHORSE and ORCHESTRA

200

CONFERENCE

201

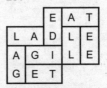

202

A	I	D	E	■	R	O	A	R
■	N	■	W	O	O	■	F	■
F	A	C	E	■	U	N	T	O
■	U	■	■	■	G	■	E	■
I	D	E	A	■	H	I	R	E
■	I	■	R	■	■	■	N	■
O	B	O	E	■	S	O	O	N
■	L	■	N	E	E	■	O	■
F	E	T	A	■	E	O	N	S

203

B	I	F	F	A	F	E	W	A
O	V	E	R	S	I	G	H	T
A	Y	Z	Y	P	X	G	O	E

204

1 Jordan, 2 Chisel, 3 Cousin, 4 Bucket,
5 Deduct, 6 Insect.
Item of sports equipment: DISCUS

Solutions

205

G	L	A	R	E
R	O	M	A	N
A	V	O	I	D
D	E	N	S	E
E	D	G	E	D

206

S	A	R	I	B	A	R	B	A	F	A	R
F	I	L	M	S	M	U	G	Y	O	G	I
D	U	M	P	L	E	V	Y	W	R	E	N
H	A	L	O	B	L	E	W	B	E	R	G
L	I	A	R	F	I	Z	Z	W	I	L	L
C	Y	S	T	R	O	C	K	O	G	L	E
C	O	M	A	B	R	I	M	I	N	C	A
L	A	W	N	G	A	S	P	L	E	N	D
Z	I	N	C	S	T	Y	E	U	R	G	E
B	L	U	E	D	E	C	K	U	S	E	R

207

CALF

Two of either E, F, T and/or A are in the solution (line 2). If both E and A are in, then so are C and S (line 5), which isn't possible (1). If both F and T are in, then A isn't (2); nor are C or S (5), which isn't possible (1). So there's one of E and A and one of F and T (2), so also (5) one of C and S. Also there's one of C and T (3), so one of S and F (5). If both R and C are in, then A isn't (1), so (above) E is in, which (4) isn't possible. If neither R nor C is in the solution, then T is (above), as are A and S (1), which (4) isn't possible. So there's exactly one of R or C. If S is in, then (above) F isn't, so T is in, C isn't (5), R is in (above), A isn't (1), so E is in (2). But then the letter in 1st position isn't E (2), T (3) or R (4), so S - and line 5 doesn't work. So S isn't in the solution, thus (above) C is in, T isn't, and R isn't. F is in the solution (5). A is in the solution (1) and there's no E (2), so L is in (4). C isn't in 3rd (1), 4th (3) or 2nd position (4), so 1st. F is in 4th position (5). A isn't in 3rd (3), so 2nd position. L is in 3rd position.

208

1 Respite, 2 Priest, 3 Tripe, 4 Pert, 5 Taper, 6 Entrap, 7 Panther.

209

The five-letter word is: CRANE

210

BANDIT, CONDOR, GANDER, RANDOM, SUNDAY, TANDEM

211

O	R	B	I	T
R	H	I	N	E
B	I	L	G	E
I	N	G	O	T
T	E	E	T	H

212

B	L	M	S	W
U	U	A	P	H
L	R	S	A	I
L	C	T	N	P
D	H	I	I	P
O	E	F	E	E
G	R	F	L	T

213

1 Astray, 2 Strain, 3 Nation, 4 Thrust, 5 Jigsaw, 6 Ignore.
Answer: TROJAN

214

1 Immense, 2 Samovar, 3 Admiral, 4 Andorra, 5 Century, 6 Attempt, 7 Shallow, 8 Impulse, 9 Mercury, 10 October, 11 Vatican.
Isaac Asimov: *Pebble in the Sky*

215

GRASS

Comparing lines 1 and 4, I is not in the solution. Comparing lines 1 and 6, M is not in the solution. Comparing lines 3 and 4, U is not in the solution, so S is correctly placed in 5th position (4). E is not in the solution (5). If H is in 1st position (6), then the letter correctly placed in line 2 is R, and there is no A (2) or T (1). But then G is in 3rd position (3) and there is no remaining incorrectly placed letter in line 3. So H is not in 1st position. In line 6, the correctly placed letter is S in 4th position, so

Solutions

there are two Ss in the solution and no H. The letter in 1st position isn't R (1) or A (3), so R is in 2nd position (2) and A is in 3rd. T isn't in the solution (1). G is in the solution (3), so in 1st position.

216
BLINDFOLD, DEMOCRACY, TYPICALLY, HOROSCOPE, GEOMETRIC, IMPERIOUS, VIEWPOINT, ZIRCONIUM.
The phrase is: IMPROPER FRACTION

217
1 Marsupial, 2 Energetic, 3 Australia, 4 Sandstorm, 5 Lightning, 6 Bethlehem, 7 Important, 8 Octagonal, 9 Trembling.

218

S	A	L	O	N		B	L	E	A	T
I		O		I			I			O
X		O		G		N	E	C	K	
T	O	M	A	H	A	W	K			E
H		I		T		A	S	P	E	N
		N		J		T		I		
D	O	G	M	A		C		Q		C
E			A	R	C	H	D	U	K	E
L	A	Z	Y		F		A			D
V		B			U		N			A
E	A	G	E	R		L	A	T	E	R

219

	I	T	C	H
S		H		O
C	L	U	M	P
A		M		E
R	U	B	Y	

220

P	S	Y	C	H	I	C
S	A	W	M	I	L	L
H	I	R	S	U	T	E
C	A	P	S	U	L	E
S	E	T	T	L	E	R
P	E	R	P	L	E	X
R	I	V	A	L	R	Y

221

R	U	E	F	U	L
S	P	O	U	S	E
P	R	I	S	O	N
B	O	X	I	N	G
C	A	V	O	R	T
D	R	E	N	C	H

222
1 Gum, 2 North, 3 Neptune, 4 Indelible, 5 Accelerated, 6 Administrator.
The word is: TURTLES

223
1 Rosemary, 2 Borage, 3 Marjoram, 4 Paprika, 5 Ginger, 6 Cinnamon, 7 Bergamot, 8 Peppermint, 9 Oregano, 10 Parsley, 11 Cardamom, 12 Tarragon.

224

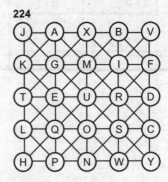

225
LOYAL
Only one of R, U, B, E or L is in the solution (line 5). So in line 4, A must be used to have three letters from that line. If O is not in the solution, then U is used (3), which eliminates R, B, E and L (5) leaving line 4 with only A, which doesn't appear three times in line 4. So O is in the solution and E and D are not (6). A and Y are in the solution (1), so U isn't (3). If P is in the solution (2), then there's no L, so two Ys are in the solution (1), together with O and A (above). But then line 5 down's work. So P is not in the solution. There aren't two Os in the solution (3), so L is in the solution in 5th position (5) and R and B are not in the solution. O is in 2nd position (2) and A is in 4th position (4). The letter in the correct position in line 1 is L in 1st position, thus so Y is in 3rd position.